When Everything's
Said & Done

When Everything's Said & Done

Eboni Snoe

sepia

BET BOOKS

BET Publications, LLC
http://www.bet.com

SEPIA BOOKS are published by

BET Publications, LLC
c/o BET BOOKS
One BET Plaza
1900 W Place NE
Washington, DC 20018-1211

All Kensington Titles, Imprints, and Distributed Lines are available at special quantity discounts for bulk purchases for sales promotions, premiums, fund-raising, and educational or institutional use. Special book excerpts or customized printings can also be created to fit specific needs. For details, write or phone the office of the Kensington special sales manager: Kensington Publishing Corp., 850 Third Avenue, New York, NY 10022, attn: Special Sales Department, Phone: 1-800-221-2647.

Library of Congress Card Catalogue Number: 2004105348
ISBN: 1-58314-341-6

First Printing: November 2004
10 9 8 7 6 5 4 3 2 1

Printed in the United States of America

To my parents, Willie Williams and Ruby Thomas Coleman Williams.
I thank you for giving me physical life.
I thank you for giving me all the love you could give.
Love lasts an eternity.

When Everything's
Said & Done

Chapter 1

Nebia's Story . . .

"**G**od couldn't be a woman. If He was, He wouldn't have created old age and menopause." Cynthia ran her hand over her loose belly as she danced. "I can't stand getting old. Every time I come over here to visit Mama, and I see that old woman who lives next door"—she thumbed toward an adjoined apartment—"it reminds me of what I can look forward to. That woman looks like something that belongs in a tomb."

"Say what?" Erica laughed.

"You know I'm not lying." Cynthia stopped dancing. "This Florida sunshine must have been hell on her complexion. So you better watch out, Erica." She nudged her sister, Sheila, jokingly. "Because you're the oldest of the group at thirty-nine, soon to see the big four-o." Cynthia gave Erica the eye. "I'm already on the job at the tender age of thirty-seven, using every cream known to man. And I'm educating Sheila here, because she'll be thirty-seven next year."

"Don't worry about my skin," Sheila replied. "And you better not let Mama hear you say that about that woman. You know she likes her."

"I know." Cynthia rolled her eyes. "She's been living in this apartment for five years and she's always talking about what Nubia said, or whatever her name may be. Some of that stuff—" Cynthia waved with disbelief. "You know that woman is lying. But Mama eats it all up."

"I know," Sheila agreed. "Like that story about the folks who used to live in this building. She told Mama some diabetic woman in a wheelchair, who owned this building, she and her pregnant daughter had it out with some gangsters in one of these apartments." Sheila's voice rose with incredulity. "This was a black woman who she claimed owned this building back then. But of course Mama believes every word of it. She was talking about how brave the people were."

The women laughed.

"And then she had the nerve"—Cynthia shook her head—"to say one of the daughters ended up living with some tribe in the Amazon, or something like that."

They started to laugh again but a husky voice interrupted them from the dark porch a few yards away. "You're talkin' about the Robinson family. Laura Robinson did own this building. Her mother willed it to her. A white man that she had a long-term relationship with bought it for her." When the voice stopped even the air seemed still. "And Cora didn't go to the Amazon. She went to Africa. South Africa."

The women stopped laughing and tried to see through the darkness. Seconds later the clouds parted overhead, transforming the moon into a giant spotlight that focused on a figure in a rocking chair.

"I'm sorry, Miss Nubia. We didn't—"

"It's Nebia," the thin woman replied.

"I mean Miss Nebia." Sheila put her hand over her heart. "We didn't know you were out here."

"So you meant to talk about me behind my back?"

"Why no, ma'am." Cynthia struggled with the right answer. "We just—"

"Why did you stop your dancing?" Nebia ignored her answer. "Dancing is a good thing to do on Midsummer's Eve. When I was younger I used to always dance when the summer solstice came. Sometimes Cora would join me. She was the only one of the Robinson girls that would." Nebia paused. "Perhaps it was because she was born on a Midsummer's Eve. Yes. Midsummer's Eve has always been special to me." The sound of the rocking chair against the wooden porch grated with a steady rhythm. "That's one reason I knew Cora would be special. But there were other reasons. One in particular. You know where the Vinoy Hotel sits now?"

Cynthia looked at Sheila and Erica out of the corner of her eyes. "Yes, ma'am."

"Back then some of downtown St. Petersburg looked a lot like it looks today with The Pier and all. There was water as far as the eye could see, but there was also a wharf."

"Really?" Cynthia rolled her eyes.

"One day when Cora was ten years old she fell off into that water. And Cora couldn't swim, and neither could me or Miss Laura, her mama. So when she went down for the third time and didn't come up, we was all in a panic. Then Miss Laura saw Big Willie coming toward us, and we screamed for him and told him Cora was drowning. I swear it was at least five minutes before he pulled that child from that water. We all thought she was dead. Back then we didn't know nothing about no CPR." Nebia nodded her head as she spoke. "Well I tell you, all on her own Cora laid up on that wharf and started coughing and spitting until she cleared her lungs and opened her eyes. And it wasn't long before she was able to talk again, and then Cora told us she was all right. I knew then she had been blessed by Yemaya, the goddess of the water, and that her life would flow just as freely as water flows on this earth, turbulence and all."

The porch went quiet.

"Uh-huh," Sheila finally said as she gave Nebia an uncertain look. "Well, we didn't mean to disturb you, Miss Nebia. We'll just go back inside." She moved towards the door. Erica and Cynthia attempted to do the same. "I'll turn the music down so we won't disturb you."

"And I also knew that Cora's appeal to men would also be strong," Nebia continued as if she didn't hear her, "because Yemaya is also the goddess of sexuality and fertility. It can be a positive thing to have men love you like that, but it can also be a burden."

"What do you mean?" Just the mention of men turned the tide of Cynthia's attention.

"When the Yoruba Orisha, Yemaya, is strong within you, it makes you a very sensuous woman."

"Yemaya . . ." Cynthia repeated the name. "The way my luck's been running I think I could use a little of that!" she said teasingly.

"I know that's right," Erica chimed in. "Finding a man has been tough. Finding a good one that's crazy about you is nearly impossible."

"Oh-h-h." Nebia stopped rocking for the first time. "You're only thinking about how good it would be."

"Why not?" Sheila replied. "If it's going to help me have it like that." Then she spoke under her breath, "Not that I really need the help."

"There she goes," Cynthia mumbled, "and here every one of us is over thirty-five, *and* alone."

"There is nothing wrong with that," Nebia said softly. "But in some women the feminine energy is extremely strong. And if it strikes one man here"—she touched where her heart lay within her bony chest—"and it is the same man that has touched the hearts of your blood sisters, it is not so good."

"I can believe that." Cynthia looked at Sheila.

"Cora had sisters too." Nebia acknowledged the direction of Cynthia's gaze.

"I guessed as much," Sheila said. "How many sisters did she have?"

"There were three of them just like you."

"I'm not their sister," Erica announced.

"Erica's not our blood sister." Cynthia motioned. "But we've been close friends for more than twenty years. So she's just like a sister."

"I can imagine," Nebia replied. "There were three Robinson girls," she continued. "Brenda was the oldest. She was a good-looking girl who always had her head in a book and had an idea where she wanted to go, but Brenda thought she knew what was best for everybody else. And then there was Annette, the youngest." Nebia tugged on one of her grey, spongy plaits and stopped rocking. "Dear, sweet Annette. If everybody saw the world the way she saw it, we would have what the Christians call heaven right here on earth."

"You're not a Christian?" Erica asked.

"I think I am. Still, some folks may not agree with me. But I believe in God, and eventually Cora believed too." She began to rock again. "We grew quite close through the years, Cora and I. You see, she was the middle child. But she came into this world looking at things differently from her sisters; still, that don't mean they weren't close. They were mighty close, at least in the beginning," Nebia said, breathing in and out slowly. "But I don't mean to take up you all's time with my ramblings. Go on back to what you were doing. Go on." Nebia became quiet, but continued to rock.

"No, it's all right." Sheila pulled a chair closer to Nebia's side of the porch. "This sounds interesting, considering Yemaya and all."

"It really does," Cynthia agreed. She sat on top of the rail that divided the porch with wide toothed slats. "Mama told us this stuff happened pretty recently."

"Yes, it wasn't that long ago," Nebia agreed. "It wasn't that long ago at all."

Chapter 2

1971 . . .

The steady click of a metal fan in the window added a unique beat to the gospel tune playing on the radio, but Laura Robinson didn't hear it. She heard the singing, alright, but she didn't hear the ticking. She was too accustomed to hearing it to hear it. What she was aware of was the sound of her daughters moving about upstairs as they prepared for Sunday service, and they weren't moving fast enough for her.

"Brenda," she called, "you all aren't ready yet? It's almost a quarter 'til." Laura walked into the kitchen and turned off the oven that held the roast she was cooking for Sunday dinner. She moved the black, crusty roaster aside to make room for the pot of okra and tomatoes, and the macaroni and cheese she had baked earlier, so the food would keep warm until they returned from service.

"Annette and I are ready, Mama, but I told Cora she can't wear what she's got on to church," Brenda announced as she walked down the stairs.

"What did you say?" Laura asked as she shifted the pans. Her words mixed with the heat and tempting smells from inside the oven. Satisfied, she straightened up and wiped her hands on her apron before she untied it and hung it on a nail. Afterwards she went into the living room. By then Cora and Annette were standing beside Brenda.

"Cora! What's got into you, girl? You can't wear that see-through dress to church without a slip. I can see every bit of your underwear."

"But it's so hot outside, Mama. And it's even hotter in that doggone church. Need to get an air conditioner," she mumbled.

"Don't talk about the Lord's house like that, Cora Robinson. And I don't care how hot it is. No daughter of mine is setting one foot outside dressed like you're dressed today, and especially going to church. Now get back upstairs and get a slip on. Right now."

Cora did as she was told and returned downstairs solemn-faced.

"Now"—Laura walked over and patted Cora on the cheek—"you look absolutely beautiful. "Let's go." She herded her daughters out the front door.

"It's a shame people can't be above that kind of thing," Annette proclaimed for Brenda and Cora's ears only as they walked down the stairs. "Why do people have to look at things in such a bad way? They all know we wear bras and panties."

"Yeah, Cora." Brenda buddied up to her younger sister. "I gotta tell you, you did look kinda sexy. And although Mama won't let us have a boyfriend, I bet that boy, Dennis Thomas, would have liked it."

But Cora remained sullen as they walked out onto the sidewalk.

"Good morning, Nebia. How you doing today?" Laura called as she spotted her long-time tenant hanging flowers and herbs upside down to dry.

"I'm just fine, Laura."

"We're on our way to church. Care to join us this morning?"

"Nope, I wouldn't."

"I knew you'd say that, but I thought I'd ask anyway," Laura replied with a smile, never breaking her stride.

Brenda and Annette waved, but Cora just looked reproachful as they continued down the street toward Ebenezer Baptist Church, their white, blue, and yellow dresses reflecting the bright Florida sun.

With unhappy eyes Cora looked at Nebia and their gazes held. Finally, Nebia tilted her chin skyward and gave Cora a reassuring look. Cora responded with a weak smile.

"There goes Warren," Brenda pointed as the boy rode his bike toward them on the opposite side of the street. "He must have gone to the corner grocery to get some eggs and bacon for breakfast."

They waved. Warren moved the small grocery sack to the crook of his arm to free one of his hands. He waved back enthusiastically.

"Mama, why don't you ever ask Warren and Miss Lucille to come to church like you ask Miss Nebia?" Annette said. "Miss Nebia always says no, and you don't even ask Miss Lucille."

"I have asked them, baby, but they choose not to come."

"But Warren has told me he'd like to come," Annette protested.

"Annette, have you ever seen any white people at our church?" Cora asked.

"No."

"Don't you get it? Warren's mother Lucille is white, and they don't want white people at our church," Cora continued.

"That's not true, Cora," her mother replied.

"Well, why don't any white people come?" Cora insisted.

"It's just that they don't feel comfortable," Brenda explained.

"How do you know?" Cora said, rolling her eyes.

"I just know," Brenda retorted.

"But Miss Lucille feels comfortable enough living in the apartment in back of us, and we're black," Annette rationalized. "Plus, Warren's father is black."

"But that's different," Brenda stated matter-of-factly. "It's because Warren's father is black that she's living behind us. I don't think she'd be accepted by her own folks."

"Just like white people wouldn't be accepted at Ebenezer," Cora added as they joined a crowd of people making their way to the double doors.

Annette looked discouraged. "I don't think it's right. Nobody's special in God's eyes. Everybody's the same. And you know people don't think Warren is white anyway."

"Shhh . . ." Laura pressed her index finger against her lips. "Now, that's enough of that talk. You all go find a seat inside the church." She advised once they made it inside, "I'm supposed to help out today, so I'll join you shortly." Laura watched Brenda, Cora, and Annette walk down front and take a seat in the second pew. Afterwards she headed toward the church offices.

Laura liked the way she felt when she was in the Lord's house. Ebenezer was a holy place, made that much more special because of the people she had come to know: the Reverend and Mrs. Parker, the deacons, and the Mothers of Ebenezer, as well as the rest of the members. Laura hoped to hold a titled position in the church one day. It was a small congregation and she looked at it as her extended family.

The office door was open and Laura entered without hesitation. Service would start soon, so she made a beeline for the closet where the collection baskets were kept. Laura stepped inside the closet that was lined with shelves full of things that made church life easier. She saw the baskets stacked in a familiar corner. She reached for them as voices came through the thin clapboard walls. Laura stood still when she heard crying.

"What are you saying?" the question was interspersed with sniffs.

"I'm simply saying, Sister Matthews, that your daughter must have misunderstood Reverend Parker's actions."

"Misunderstood?" Sister Matthews' voice rose. "I don't know how else she was suppose to take it. She said he put his hand on her breast, squeezed it, then tried to kiss her."

"Now, Sister Matthews—"

"And then when she told Reverend Parker to stop, he told her he didn't know why she was protesting 'cause he could tell from the way she was messin' around with some of the boys in the church that she was letting them do the same thing."

"Now wait a minute, Sis—"

"And when she *insisted* he stop, Reverend got angry and told her he didn't want her no way. She said he said, 'Why would I mess with hamburger when I can go after steak like Cora Robinson?'"

Laura nearly knocked the baskets over when she heard her fourteen-year-old daughter's name.

"Sister Matthews, you gon' have to calm down." The deacon's voice was no longer friendly. "You can't go around making accusations like that against somebody unless you got proof."

"My daughter's word is my proof."

"Well. You know you're forcing me to say this." There was a moment of silence. "She does have quite a reputation in the neighborhood, and some of that is your fault."

"What?"

"I've heard you let her go to that tavern next door to your house."

"Yes, she has gone over there in the daytime to get a soda when they are preparing to open for business later on, but she's never been in Lucky's while it was selling liquor."

"Can you say so much for yourself?" The words were full of accusation.

"Pardon me?"

"I said, can you swear on the Bible that since you've been a member of Ebenezer, that you have never been over in that devil's playhouse drinking with the rest of them folks? And we all know what goes on in them dark corners outside of drinking."

"Well, I-I . . ." Sister Matthews stumbled.

"Now look, Sister Matthews," the deacon's voice turned placating again, "I don't want to bring up all this unpleasantness. So, let's just forget about the whole thing, and none of you will have to be brought down front to face the congregation."

Laura heard crying again. That was enough for her. She left the baskets where they were.

Laura was shaking when she left the church office. At first she walked slowly as if she were in a daze. But the more Laura thought about what she had overheard, the faster she went. When Laura entered the church hall Reverend Parker was taking the mic. His strong bass voice boomed above the rest of the congregation as the service opened with a hymn. "I want to be more and more like Jesus every day. So meek and lowly, so high and holy. I want to be more and more like Jesus every day."

Laura didn't take her eyes off of the Reverend as she marched down to where her daughters sat. The closer she got the more she locked into Reverend Parker's gaze, until finally she stood before him. In a voice loud enough for everybody to hear, Laura said, "If I ever hear that you have even tried to put your hands on one of my girls, you're going to need God and the devil to get me off of you." The church went as quiet as a tomb. Then Laura turned to Brenda, Annette, and Cora and said, "Let's go home." She walked out of Ebenezer with a confused Annette, bewildered Brenda, and an impressed Cora behind her.

Nebia's Story . . .

Cynthia swatted at a mosquito. "I can see myself doing something just like that if I thought some old man was trying to mess with a child of mine. Preacher or not." She huffed then added softly, "That is, if I had children."

"I can, too," Sheila seconded her. "Man I wish I could have seen the looks on the folks' faces in that church."

"Laura never set foot in that church again," Nebia said, her voice low. "But the girls . . . now, that's a different story. Annette became deeply religious and Brenda attended church regularly." She paused. "Just last year the old Ebenezer Church building was demolished, and a new brick building went up four blocks away."

"I don't think she should have stopped going to church," Erica said. "Miss Laura should have told the girl's father and let him handle it." A mischievous look crossed her face. "I've never heard of a preacher getting beat up in his own church before."

"But there's a first time for everything." Cynthia laughed.

"In all the years that I've lived here"—Nebia patted her hands—"and that's been forty-something years because I moved in right before Cora was born, I saw Steven Robinson twice. He had his own set of problems, and he was just too restless to stay around a house with a woman and three girls. I think Cora got some of her restlessness from her daddy."

"So he left them?" Sheila asked.

"You could say that, although the truth is he was never really with them," Nebia replied. "He was gone all the time. Steven just kinda came and went until he stopped doing that."

"I wonder if that messed with them . . . the girls. You know what I mean? Mama always said we wouldn't have had so much mouth if our father had lived to see us grown."

Nebia pursed her lips. "I believe it affected them. Yes, I surely do. I say that because Brenda tried to become the father after he really left. Then Annette, she wanted to make everything perfect because she felt her life wasn't. And Cora . . ." Nebia shook her head. "Cora wasn't afraid of anything. Cora was a treasure chest that could come up with whatever everybody needed. And she was Laura's favorite because of it. Everybody knew that."

Chapter 3

"I told you if you ever messed with Annette again"—Cora walked up on the girl after school—"I was going to kick your ass. So you think she's crazy cuz she carries a Bible around and tries to change fools like you. Well, I'm gon' show you crazy." Cora grabbed the girl's head at the base of her two fake afro puffs and pulled it down. Then she kneed her between her legs. The girl fell with Cora on top of her whaling away. One of the afro puffs was in her fist. A crowd gathered around them, and the only voice that seemed able to penetrate Cora's rage was Brenda's as she pulled at her shoulders.

"That's enough, Cora. I said that's enough." Brenda wouldn't let her go. "We better get out of here before the principal or one of the teachers comes."

Cora got up and dropped the afro puff on the ground beside the girl. "So I guess you won't break nobody else's glasses," she announced as she patted her own afro into place, pulled down her ribbed T-shirt and dusted off her elephant leg pants.

The crowd was hashing over the results of the fight when Brenda and Cora passed by as they headed home. Annette was already there.

She had gotten out of school early for a doctor's appointment. Her eyes grew large when she saw Cora.

"How did you get that big scratch on your face?" she asked when they walked through the door.

"She beat that girl up that broke your glasses," Brenda replied.

"No you didn't!" Annette proclaimed.

"Humph! Yes I did," Cora said. "I held back when she said all that stuff about you and when she put that chewed-up food in your hair. But, Annette, she broke the camel's back when she broke your glasses."

"Cora-a! I'm fourteen years old, and I don't need you going around beating people up for me. That's exactly what I don't want anyone doing. Fighting and hurting one another."

"Well it's too late now cuz you can believe she's hurt," Brenda said, bowing her head. Then she started to laugh. "And I thought I'd die when Cora dropped her afro puff on the ground beside her."

"You mean her hair came off?" Annette's eyes opened wider.

"Not only did it come off," Brenda said in stitches, "but Cora was beating the girl with the hairpiece still in her hand."

Annette looked at Cora. Cora looked at Annette, and they burst out laughing. The three of them laughed until they cried. They laughed until Annette started to prance in order not to wet herself.

"Uh-oh." Cora stopped suddenly. "Here comes Mama. How did she get off from work so early?"

"I don't know, but you know she doesn't want us fighting," Brenda reminded her. "And here you are, sixteen, doing it." She made a noise. "What are you going to tell her about that scratch on your face?"

"I don't know, but I'll think of something." Cora watched through the sheers as her mother approached their sidewalk.

"You better hurry up because here she comes." Apprehension was all over Annette's face.

"I'm going up to Nebia's." Cora headed for the back door. "You all tell Mama that Nebia promised to show me some new things with her herbs."

"Look, I'm not about to start lying to Mama," Annette said. "I'll tell her you're over there but that's all."

"Well, I guess that's going to have to do," Cora said as she came back and mushed her sister's cheeks. "When it gets dark enough I'll come to the screen door and tell Mama Nebia's invited me to dinner. That way, by the time she really sees the scar tomorrow, Nebia and I will have it well on its way to being healed."

Cora went out the door and squeezed through the slats that divided their porch from Nebia's. She tapped on the screen door but didn't wait for an answer before she went inside.

"It's me, Nebia. Where are you?"

"I'm right here."

Cora followed Nebia's voice to the kitchen. "What you doing?"

Nebia kept her back turned. "I'm fixin' up a poultice for Mrs. Winfrey down the street."

"What's in it?" Cora leaned in for a look.

"You tell me," Nebia replied.

Cora studied the herbs that were piled into the center of the small linen square. Then she leaned over closer and smelled it. "I'd say garlic, burdock, and goldenseal."

"That's right, but you missed this right here." Nebia nudged some dark green crumbled bits of dried leaves with her index fingertip. "That's comfrey."

"Oh. Okay." Cora looked behind her. "Nebia, can I break off a piece of your aloe plant, to put on this scratch?"

Nebia looked at Cora's face for the first time. "After you put some tea tree oil on it." She went back to the poultice. Nebia closed it then tied it with string. "You been fighting?"

"Yeah, I've been fighting." Cora heaved a sigh. She looked at the new poultice. "You're going to tell me I'm wrong?"

"No. I'm not going to tell you that."

"No?" Cora was surprised. With a spring in her step she went over to the cabinet where Nebia kept her oils.

"There is no wrong, the way I see it," Nebia continued. "But there are choices, and all choices have consequences. You may have been fighting for something you thought was right, but whatever choices you make, make sure you are prepared for the consequences. In this case that means the scratch on your face, and hiding out from your mama until the redness is out of it so she won't know that you've been fighting. But remember, Cora, as you get older the choices will become more serious and so will the consequences," Nebia warned.

Cora spent the rest of the afternoon helping Nebia grind herbs into powders, and bundling up small bouquets of dried lavender, sage, and peppermint. With Laura's permission, they enjoyed a companionable meal, and Cora did the dishes.

"Nebia. Why do you always say there is no wrong when the whole world knows things like smoking and drinking and having sex when you're not married is?" Cora asked as she folded up the drying towel.

"I guess I look at things a little differently from most folks. I think there's a danger in believing that God, or the forces of God, are only one way. God is in everything because He created every-thing. If God doesn't know about it, then who does?"

"The devil."

"But you see, I believe Satan, if you believe in Him, is a tool of God's. How would you know what light is without the dark, and how would you know what beauty is without ugliness? You need them both, Cora. And if God is *the* creator, He created all of it. And how could God create anything wrong?"

Cora nodded, but her brow furrowed as she thought about Nebia's words.

"It's all about choices, Cora. God has laid out a plan, but it looks like a maze to us. All of us aren't gon' make the best choices for our highest good every time, but there's always another chance. We're done when we finally make the choices that bring us true happiness, and that prove to us how much we are like our creator, like God."

"Is that why we're here?" Cora hung up the drying towel.

"I believe that's the reason. Some of us go about it with more passion than others, but it doesn't make them better or worse. We are all equal in God's eyes."

Cora nodded again. "Thanks for dinner and for the aloe."

"You're welcome."

"Good night," Cora said as she opened the door.

"'Night, Cora."

Cora stepped onto the back porch and looked up at the moon. She stood there for some time wondering about the things Nebia had said.

"Hey Cora," a voice called. "I heard you whipped up on that Mason girl pretty good today."

Cora looked over into the empty lot next door and saw Warren coming home through a path lined with weeds.

"Be quiet, boy. My mama or your mama might hear you." She walked down the stairs. "And you know if Lucille finds out she's going to tell Laura."

"Boy? Who you calling boy?"

"I don't see nobody out here who would fit that description besides you."

"I got your boy, all right." He sat down on the step beside her feet. "I'm going into boot camp in two months. I don't know what you're talking about."

"No you're not, Warren," Cora looked down at the curly head she had known for so long.

"Yes, I am. It's all settled."

"I don't know why I'm so shocked. I never thought you would join the service."

"What did you think I was going to do? I'm not exactly your best student. And my mama don't have no money for me to go to college."

"I don't know what I thought," Cora replied quietly, sitting down beside him. "Things are really changing. Brenda graduates this summer. She'll be eighteen next month. And in the fall she goes off to Florida A&M. I never thought about a time when Annette, Brenda, and me wouldn't be together."

"Well, what do you plan to do when you graduate next year?" Warren asked.

Cora looked at the sky. "I've got so many things I want to do. I want to see other people and places. I want to paint. Perhaps I'll even open up my own flower shop one day."

"You're not going to college like Brenda?" Warren watched a firefly land on the stair rail.

"No." Cora rubbed her thigh. "Brenda got a scholarship. Besides, she already knows what she wants to be."

"What's that?" Warren asked.

"A sociologist."

"That sounds like Brenda."

They turned quiet.

"Why don't you join the WAC, Cora? That way you'll get to travel and learn some skills to support yourself."

"I don't think so." Cora squinted. "The army is not for me. Now, think about it. Can you see me in one of those uniforms? All crisp and neat and obeying all those rules?" She threw her head back and laughed.

Warren looked at her, but turned away before Cora saw the admiration in his eyes. "I think you'd look good in a uniform." He made the words sound casual.

"You do?" She scrunched up her nose.

Warren nodded and kicked a candy wrapper near his foot.

"Well, you're about the only one," Cora replied. "Nope. I can't wear nobody's uniform. I've got to be free to wear whatever I please, whenever it pleases me." She wriggled her shoulders suggestively.

"Don't do that."

"Don't do what?"

"You know. Act like that."

"Like what, Warren? Like those girls I see you messing around with after school? You seem to like it when they do it."

"Well, that's different. They're not you." He paused. "You're special."

"I am?" Cora looked at him.

"Yeah. You are."

"And how's that?"

"You don't have to do the things that girls consciously do to get a guy's attention. Just the way you are naturally gets his attention."

"Is that right?" Cora smiled.

"Yeah, it's right." Warren leaned forward. "And you know it, too."

"No I don't." Cora sighed. "You know, it's so confusing. Some days I want to be like Sheila Frazier or some of those other sexy women I see in the movies. Then on other days I feel like I felt today, full of hell and wanting to take it out on folks who like dishing it out but can't really take it."

"I think everybody feels like that sometimes," Warren said.

"Everybody except for Annette." Cora laughed, then she sighed again. "We've had some good times around here, haven't we?"

"Mm-hmm."

"It was always you and me playing tricks on Brenda and Annette. It's funny how things that made them crazy didn't bother me a bit."

"Yeah. You were a good partner, Cora. I'm going to miss you."

Cora patted her thighs and eased up off the step. "I'm going to miss you too, Warren. For the first time I realize I'm going to miss a lot of things around here."

Nebia's Story . . .

Nebia coughed. "Cora's thoughts and desires were like an underground stream, powerful enough to cut their way but still needing a place to surface."

"What d'ya mean, Miss Nebia?" Sheila asked.

"She had so much going on inside her, things that a lot of young people don't give a second thought to. Cora didn't want to think about them but they were there vying for her attention. She couldn't see that Warren cared for her in a special way. And even if she had seen it, it wouldn't have mattered because she was on a journey of self-discovery that wouldn't allow anybody in besides her family or me."

"So did Warren go off to boot camp?" Cynthia had to know.

"Yes, he did. And Brenda went to college and got a degree in sociology, and Cora went her own way traveling and living in different cities, making a living off of her paintings and flowers. She would take an odd job here and there if it suited her. But basically she lived as she wanted. Somehow she managed to do that even if it meant staying with a man that took her fancy, or living in one of those communes that were still plentiful back in the seventies."

"You mean Cora would live with a man just so that she could have a place to sleep?" Erica asked with disapproval.

"Nooo . . ." Nebia drew the sound out long and deep. "She had to fancy him. Cora had to want him as bad as he wanted her, but for Cora there always came a time when enough was enough, and she would leave."

"So she would live with him, have sex with him, then leave whenever she got ready?"

"That's about it."

"M-m-m. I don't know about that," Erica said. "She sounds like a mighty loose woman to me."

"Well, those were the choices that Cora made. And she seemed to be happy. But things changed when Michael Dawson moved into this building and starting living in the efficiency upstairs."

"Is that the man that messed up everything?" Cynthia asked.

"I wouldn't say that," Nebia replied. "It was certainly not his intention. But life has a strange way of unfolding at times. It might have been simpler if Michael had never come to this area when he was looking for a job. Or maybe if he and Brenda had gotten together the first time she saw him at the college party and liked what she saw. You see, Michael attended Florida A&M when Brenda was there. But it just didn't happen that way."

Chapter 4

"Nobody's gonna come. I don't have nothing but old folks and little kids in the backyard," Annette complained as she and Brenda stood on the sidewalk in front of their house.

She glanced back at the Robinsons' backyard that looked like a carnival with large colorful Christmas lights strung from tree to tree and balloons dangling everywhere. An extension cord ran out of Nebia's kitchen window to power the record player that sat on a card table in the middle of stacks and stacks of forty-fives. The frappe was still fresh with lumps of orange sherbet floating in a sea of ginger ale. There were cookies and cake and fried chicken piled high on a platter beside a dish of deviled eggs. And there were gifts, for what would a graduation party be without them?

"What are you talking about?" Brenda asked. "There are plenty of young people back there."

"Yeah, I know." Annette sighed. "But not the right people."

"You're thinking about that guy Michael that lives upstairs again."

"Yes I am. He said his trip would only take a couple of days, and he promised if he didn't make it back in time for the graduation ceremony that he would definitely make it to my party."

"He still can, Annette. It's early," Brenda reassured her. "Listen." She stopped and cocked her head to the side. "Isn't that—It is! That's ''Til I Reach The Highest Ground,' your favorite. Let's go back there and join everybody else."

They turned toward the house but the beam of car headlights turning onto their street stopped them. It was a string-bean green Nova, and it came to a halt right at the end of their sidewalk.

"Who's that?" Annette asked.

"How am I suppose to know? I haven't been back in St. Pete but a couple of days. You don't know anybody with a green Nova?"

"Uh-uh," Annette replied.

They watched as the car sat silent; then the door opened on the passenger's side. A young man with a psychedelic shirt bent his head and climbed out.

"Who is it?" Brenda strained to see through the trees and the dark, but Annette was way ahead of her.

"Michael!" Annette nearly screamed. She ran up to him and threw her arms around his neck, then she took them down quickly and folded them in front of her. "You made it back."

"I told you I would." He smiled at her and touched her cheek.

Annette stepped back and looked at the Nova. "But whose car is this?"

"It's mine."

"Yours? You left here on the bus."

"Yep. But when I was in Memphis I went to a police auction. I was able to buy this and drive it off the lot for two hundred and fifteen dollars. And there's only one thing that I know that's wrong with it. You can't open the driver's door from the inside."

"This is unreal." Annette covered her mouth and started laughing. Then she looked at Michael and smiled. "Well, come on. The party is in the backyard and it's going great." She grabbed his arm and began to pull him towards the house. "Oh, Brenda," Annette said when she saw her sister standing there. "*This* is Michael."

"Hello." Michael smiled.

Brenda's mouth opened but no sound came out. Finally "hey" emerged. "Forgive me for staring but . . . didn't you attend Florida A&M?"

"Yeah." Recognition dawned in Michael's voice. "I remember you. I've seen you on campus."

"I thought so." An uncomfortable look surfaced and faded in Brenda's eyes.

Michael continued. "We hung out in different groups, but I remember one day there was this big discussion about black folks not owning any businesses in Florida. You piped up and said your family owned an apartment building here in St. Petersburg. I remembered that when I got a job here."

"Really," Brenda said, her eyes a bit too large.

"Now look-a-there." Annette tugged on Michael's arm. "Brenda was always the first one of us to spot a good-looking guy."

They laughed and walked toward the house. The clapping from the backyard was almost as loud as Stevie Wonder's singing. When they reached the back Laura was standing at the gate. She had a handful of homemade sugar cookies. Nebia stood beside her.

"Hello, Miss Laura. Miss Nebia," Michael said with respect. "I told Annette I'd be back. The party seems to be going good."

"It is," Laura said, wiping cookie crumbs from her mouth.

"Mama," Annette said softly. "I thought the doctor told you not to eat any sweets."

"This lit-a-bit of cookies is not going to hurt me," Laura replied.

"Why aren't you suppose to be eating any sweets?" Brenda's forehead wrinkled with concern.

"The doctor says I got a touch of diabetes and I just need to lose a few pounds and watch what I eat. That's all."

"Diabetes!" Brenda repeated the word as if she had never heard it before. "Why didn't anybody tell me about this?"

"Because I knew you were going to act just like you're acting now." Laura leaned toward her. "But this isn't the place or the time to talk about it." She turned to Michael. "How was Memphis?"

"Good. Memphis was good," Michael said.

"It went real good, Mama," Annette chirped. "Michael bought a car."

"Is that right? What kind did you get?"

"It's just an old Nova, Miss Laura. Something to get around in until I can get one of those small business loans I've been applying for."

"Do it, girl. Come on, now," erupted from behind them. Some of the guests had formed a semicircle on the grass. In the middle were two adolescents holding a wooden closet rod. Right now it was moonlighting as a really low limbo stick.

"All right. Here I go," Cora warned as she tied her long, white linen dress in a knot between her thighs. Cora threw her arms out and leaned back. Her smile was wide and bright as she laughed at her own antics, and the ends of her beaded cornrowed braids dangled above her shoulder blades. Cora shrieked when she couldn't bend any further. She was on her butt, but her laugh was louder than anyone else's.

"That's my sister, Cora. Fresh from L.A.," Annette explained.

Cora lifted her arms and a young man responded, pulling her up, off the ground. "Oh-h," she moaned and placed her palms against her butt cheeks, then started laughing again. Cora caught sight of her family and walked stiffly in their direction.

"Cora, when are you gon' grow up?" Laura chastised her, but there was unadulterated love in her eyes.

"I am grown, Mama." She threw an arm around her mother's shoulders and gave her a hug, then started to whimper again. "Oh, my butt."

"Is it broken?" Michael asked, smiling.

"I hope not. It's still got a long, long way to go." Cora replied.

Brenda shook her head. "Never mind her, Michael. She's always been this way. No matter how we've tried to teach her better. And since she's been living in California she's worse than ever."

"O-o-kay. So that's how it is, huh?" Cora looked Michael up and down. "I gather this is somebody I am suppose to impress."

"This is Michael, Cora." Annette gave her the eye. "The one who moved upstairs in the efficiency."

"Michael." Cora nodded her understanding. "Now I get it. All right. Let's start over." Cora turned her back to them, untied her dress and smoothed out the wrinkles. When she faced them again she offered Michael a regal hand in greeting. "How are you, Michael?"

"Just fine, thank you." He grinned.

"So you're the man who stole my baby sister's heart," she accused with a straight face.

"Cor-ra," Annette howled.

Michael let go a throaty laugh. "Is that what I've done? I hadn't heard it put that way before."

"Cora doesn't like to beat around the bush"—Brenda gave her a pinch—"no matter how rude it might be."

Cora jumped. "But of course I could always count on Brenda to let me know when I was being rude." She picked up a Styrofoam cup with ice in it and popped a small cube in her mouth. "Still, what else is family for if they can't cool you down when you need it?" With double action speed Cora dropped another ice cube down Brenda's back and flicked the water from her fingers into Annette's face before she broke into a run. Brenda and Annette dashed after her.

The party went on for a few more hours; it was almost midnight before the outdoor festivities fizzled out. Afterwards a few guests went inside and played Tunk, Spades, and Bid Whist. Then, when everyone had gone home, Brenda and Laura finished things up in the kitchen, while Cora and Annette put her graduation presents away upstairs.

"It sure is good to have all three of you here at the same time again," Laura said as she dried a Pyrex dish.

"It is good, isn't it?" Brenda took the dish from her mother and placed it in the cabinet.

"I don't know how long Cora's gon' stay this time. But you'll be here for quite a while, won't you?"

"I sure will. I've got to find me a job, though. I'm going to pick up some applications from downtown on Monday. I already applied for a job in Tampa and one in Sarasota."

"Well, you know you're welcome to stay as long as you need to. Now that Annette has graduated, I guess it won't be long before all of you are married and gone," Laura said with a distant look in her eyes.

"Lord, can you imagine Cora married with babies?" Brenda shook her head. "I can't."

"You know"—Laura thought about it—"I can. I think Cora would make a good mother if she settled down and put her mind to it. Now when will that be? That's a whole different subject. Only the Lord and Cora know." Laura looked up at the ceiling.

"Now that dress is going to look good on you, girl," Cora said as Annette hung the gift inside her closet. "Maybe you can wear it for Michael one day. Put some fire under him."

"I don't know about that."

"What do you mean you don't know? I thought you liked him."

Annette turned around slowly and looked at her sister. "I think I love him. And Cora, it's the first time I've ever been in love."

"Well isn't this a trip?" Cora replied. "This is the first time my baby sister has beat me to the punch in anything."

"You've never been in love?"

"I don't think so."

"But what about all those men you've been with? You mean you didn't love them?" She was shocked. "Fornication is a sin anyway, but to think you were fornicating and weren't even in love . . . that's worse."

"All what men? You make it sound like I've been to bed with the whole state of California."

"Well how many were there?"

Cora sat back. "You're not suppose to ask me that."

Annette looked down. "I used to could ask you anything."

"And you still can, Annie." Cora tugged at her sister's hand and made her sit down beside her. "I've had a few men"—she looked into Annette's eyes—"but not nearly as many as people would like to believe. You don't always have to sleep with a man for him to treat you good. Do things for you. You just have to make them want to."

"How do you do that?" Annette watched Cora's face intently.

"By making them believe that eventually they will sleep with you."

"But that's just as bad."

"Don't you want to sleep with Michael?"

"I thought about it, but I put it out of my mind because I'm not gonna sleep with anybody without being married to them."

"All right. There's nothing wrong with that. It might be a little boring, and you won't know the quality of the goods that you're getting until you buy them, but that's the chance that you take when you want to be holy and everything."

"I'm not trying to be holy. I just want to do the right thing in the eyes of God."

"Who knows what's in God's eyes?" Cora waved her hand. "Everything is. The hooker. The nun. The murderer and the priest."

"Oh Cora. I don't know how we see things so different. We grew up in the same house together with the same mama."

"I know how. While you were reading the Bible and taking every opportunity you could to go to that church across town, I was observing the people around me, like Nebia and that woman who was always getting into cars with different men at the corner of Seventh and Central."

"That woman was a prostitute," Annette retorted. "And some of the folks around here call Nebia a voodoo woman."

"Pleeze." Cora sucked her teeth. "Either way, I still watched and

wondered why some people saw life one way, and others saw it another. I finally decided, it's because if you never step outside the
circle of things that folks have decided you should learn, or be,
there's so much of life you miss because you make that your whole
world. I decided to step out, Annette. That's all." Cora picked up a
package of windowpane stockings. "But you know what I believe
most of all?"

"What?" Annette looked at her sister with uncertainty.

"That the world needs folks like you and like me, and all the
other people that we find to be so different. I think we balance
each other out."

"I wonder if I'll ever marry Michael." Annette fluctuated back to
the subject that dominated her thoughts.

"And if you'll ever get to have sex with him?" Cora hedged.

"Yeah." Annette laughed.

Nebia's Story . . .

"Sounds like everybody was fine to me," Cynthia concluded. "I
mean, they weren't arguing over Michael or anything."

"Everything was good for quite a while," Nebia said. "And Michael
was always in the Robinsons' apartment. Laura liked that because
that way she could keep an eye on him and Annette. Not that she
was really worried about her because Laura knew Annette was deeply
religious. But after a while, we all got the feeling that although
Michael cared for Annette, he felt she had some growing up to do,
and he wasn't about to rush her. So yes, things were real good around
here for a while." Nebia hummed softly and the women waited for
her to speak again.

"Finally Annette decided she wasn't going away for school, instead she was going to go to the local college. That was okay with
Laura, although she believed Annette might have gone out of
state if it wasn't for Michael. So Annette made preparations to
start college that fall, but she was always complaining that she

didn't feel useful just working on something that would better her own future. She felt like she should be doing more for others."

"Did she find something else?" Sheila asked. Nebia closed her eyes and sat quiet for a moment, before she said, "She most certainly did."

Chapter 5

Without looking, Cora's fingers worked at the last plait on Annette's head. Annette was seated on the floor between her legs. Both their gazes were focused on the television screen. Cora looked away to find the afro-pic. She grabbed it and started picking out Annette's hair. "This is why I got my hair braided out in L.A.," she said. "Braiding my 'fro at night and taking it down in the morning was too much work for me."

"Is it on yet?" Brenda asked as she came down the stairs with the hair grease.

Annette glanced at her. "Not yet." She looked back at the television. "But it will be on any minute now."

Then the familiar image of an animated train, puffing smoke, and moving on down the track filled the screen. "The So-o-ul Train" boomed through the set, and Cora, Brenda and Annette added their own version of, "Do-do-do-do-do-do-o Do Do!" as their favorite Saturday-morning program began.

"Do you think Don Cornelius ever gets excited?" Brenda asked as the low-key commentator appeared.

"No," Cora quickly replied. Cornelius announced Saturday's guests before another commercial began.

"When you were in L.A. did you ever try to get on *Soul Train?*" Brenda inquired as she sat down on the other end of the couch.

"I thought about it, but—"

"Hush! Hush!" Annette cut her off. "This must be that commercial that they were talking about at church a couple of weeks ago."

Cora fell silent as images of starving African babies and children with bloated stomachs filled the T.V. screen. Their eyes were devoid of life but had so much discharge that they attracted flies.

"Ah-h, that's awful," Brenda said and turned away.

"It is, isn't it?" Cora agreed.

"What is it?" Laura stepped through the front door as a familiar face appeared on the television. It was Gloria from the sitcom *All In The Family* using her real name and asking for help and donations for the needy children.

"It's horrible." Annette's voice shook. "Just horrible. We need to do something about it."

Once again the T.V. screen filled with the *Soul Train* dancers in platform shoes, hot pants, and halter tops.

"The best you can do is work on yourself," Laura said as she headed for the kitchen. "I just saw Lucille. She told me they got a letter from Warren today. He's in Germany."

"How's he do—"

"Work on ourselves!" Annette broke in. "How is that going to help those little children?" Her eyes were bright. "By the time I graduate from college they will all be dead."

"If you work on yourself, Annette"—Laura patted her breasts—"you can make sure that any children you bring into this world will have a better life than those children."

"But that's so selfish," Annette declared.

Laura looked at her daughter's pained face. "Call it what you may, but that's how it is."

Annette stood up. "Well, I won't let it be that way for me. At

Bethel Methodist they've been talking about some missionaries who are going to Zambia, South Africa. They're going in a couple of weeks." She hesitated. "And I want to go with them."

"Some missionaries!" Laura looked startled, then disgusted. "Ain't no child of mine going off to Africa working with no mission. These churches need to quit brainwashing folks. They have you believing they know the way, and the leaders can't even lead themselves to live a decent life."

"That's not true," Annette argued. "The pastor at Bethel Methodist is a good man, and so are the other people there."

"Don't tell me about what goes on at these churches, 'cause I know," Laura shot back.

"Just because that stuff happened at Ebenezer years ago it doesn't mean that's what's going on in every church. Maybe you would know that if you had found another church and continued to go like you should have."

"I'm not going to allow you to talk to me like that, Annette Robinson. And I don't want to hear any more about any missions because you are not going."

"Mama, Annette is out of high school." Brenda defended her sister. "And I think you should allow her to make her own decisions about what she wants to do with her life. There are a lot of social programs cropping up that are very good. And I believe that working with programs like the one we just saw, and with the system, is the only way things are going to get better for all of us."

"You haven't heard me say anything against the system." Laura directed her attention to Brenda. "But I do know one thing. No matter what kind of system you are working under you got to think for yourself. Keep your own eyes open and sometimes the agenda isn't as simple as it seems."

"I am thinking for myself, Mama," Annette said with tears in her eyes. "And I am going to Africa no matter what you say. Do you hear me?" She ran out the front door.

"You are so skeptical, Mama." Brenda began to shake her head. "All the world isn't out to get us."

"And *you* believe the system has all the answers. Maybe you're not skeptical enough."

Brenda's lips tightened. "How could I not be, living in this house?" She went upstairs.

Cora continued to look at her mother as she stood holding her sun hat in her hand. Their eyes met before Laura turned and went into the kitchen.

Cora went and stood on the front porch.

"I can't believe this. You don't understand me either!" Came from somewhere above. Cora walked to the edge of the house just as Annette rushed down the stairs from Michael's efficiency. She passed Cora without saying a word.

"Where you going?" Michael called.

"I don't know. I just know I need to get away from here," Annette replied.

Cora started in behind her.

"Don't follow me, Cora." Annette pinned her with glistening eyes. "I'll be okay."

"You sure?"

Annette nodded and Cora watched her sister head down the street. Michael remained at the bottom of the staircase.

"Where is she going?" He watched Annette disappear around the corner.

"I'm not sure." Cora exhaled as a powerful breeze whipped her braids into her face and a whistle began to blow.

"That's my teapot." Michael turned toward the stairs. "I was about to make a cup of instant coffee. Want some?"

Cora looked at him. "You drink coffee in the middle of the day?"

"Not usually, but I decided I needed a little pick-me-up. Come on." He beckoned.

"Okay." Cora climbed the stairs and Michael opened the door to his unit so Cora could go in.

"I didn't want to start in on the Southern Comfort this early, so I thought Maxwell House would do." He went over and picked up the kettle. Michael stared at it. "I didn't mean to upset Annette. I just told her that seeing a television commercial wasn't reason enough to become a missionary in Africa."

"It wasn't just you," Cora said. "She was already upset before she came up here."

"I figured that, but I could have been a little more sensitive and allowed her to talk it out. I guess I'm still dealing with the rejection letter I got from the SBA yesterday, and I'm not dealing with it too well."

"What's the SBA?"

"Small Business Association. I've been trying to get a loan from them so I can start my insurance business." Michael put a heaping teaspoon of coffee into a steaming cup of water and stirred as he looked out the window.

"So I guess that means you got to keep trying."

"This is the third time they've turned me down and I'm beginning to believe it's because I'm black." Michael looked at the black coffee inside his cup.

"Can't let that stop you," Cora said. "You're gonna always be black."

"I know," Michael replied. "I guess that's what's scaring me at the moment."

He turned to the window again. "It looks like it's going to storm out there. The sky is turning dark and some dangerous looking clouds are rolling in pretty fast."

Cora walked over and stood beside him. "I hope Annette has sense enough to come back if it gets too bad."

"Yeah. Seems like it might tear up something for sure." Michael spoke softly. "It looks like how I feel inside. I feel like I could walk right up to the man in charge and lay him out cold. And I don't mean the head of the SBA." Michael looked at Cora's face. "Life can be so hard, Cora. So unfair. Hell, all I want is a fair shake in this world." He closed his eyes. "Then I think about Annette and how she cares so much for others, and I think about the children in that commercial, and I feel ashamed for even wanting that."

"Michael." Cora put her arms around him. "It's alright to want more for yourself. Believe it or not, it simply means you're human." She spoke into his ear.

Michael squeezed Cora against him. "You don't know how long I've had this need to build something. To be somebody. I guess it's because when my mama died after working all her life cleaning other folks' housing and taking care of their children just so I wouldn't have to, I promised myself and her that I would succeed. And I've just got to succeed, Cora. I've got to."

Cora felt Michael's warm breath on her neck, the softness of his skin, and the hardness of his chest. They became still, and as if by telepathy pulled apart slightly. Awareness of a kind of chemistry between them was in both sets of eyes. By sheer instinct Cora turned and looked out the window. Brenda was standing there. Their gazes held as distrust dawned in Brenda's eyes.

"I thought Annette might be up here." Brenda stared at them. "But I can see I was wrong." She disappeared out of the window.

Cora stepped away. "I think I better go."

"Sure." Michael nodded.

It started to rain as Cora headed down the stairs behind Brenda. They met at the front door. Rain dripped down both of their faces.

"It's not like what you're thinking," Cora began.

"It's not?" Brenda said skeptically.

"No." Cora hugged her arms across her body.

Brenda shook her head. Rain drenched her hardened face. "You've done a lot of things, Cora. But I never thought you'd make a move on your baby sister's boyfriend."

Cora started to respond but Annette walked up the walkway. She was soaked to the skin.

"I signed up for the mission," she announced.

"You'll need some company," Brenda said. "I'm going with you."

Guilt sparked in Cora. "And you two are not going without me."

Annette put her arms around her sisters. Over her head Brenda and Cora looked at each other as small flashes of lightning lit up the sky. They echoed the tear that had come between Brenda and Cora.

Nebia's Story . . .

"I'm telling you now, Sheila," Cynthia said as she got off the rail and pulled up a chair. "If you had gone off and joined some missionary you would have gone by yourself."

"You didn't have to worry about that," Sheila replied. "That's not even my style. Sounds more like Erica to me."

"Yeah. Right," Erica said.

"That shows you how close Brenda, Cora, and Annette were," Nebia said. "They shared an unusual bond."

"So they all went to Africa?" Erica wanted to hear the rest of the story.

"Yes, they all went. And Laura was alone." Nebia paused. "The house was quiet without the girls and Michael was never there. He found a job in Tampa."

"So did they actually stay in Africa for a year?" Erica pressed.

"Not quite," Nebia laid her head against the rocking chair and looked at the sky.

Chapter 6

"I thought the supplies were suppose to get here on Friday," Cora said as she looked at the sparse shelves of canned goods and toiletries. She swiped at the flies that were attracted by the sweat running down her face. It was hot inside the makeshift supply house, but it was even hotter outside.

"I guess they didn't," Brenda replied. "But they'll probably come today."

"Now you sound like Reverend Pete. That's what he told me two weeks ago." Cora picked up the last half bar of soap. "I hope we don't end up washing our butts with leaves and pretending their slickness is lather."

Brenda shrugged. "Hey, the supplies are late, but they got to get here sometime." She took the bag of peppermint. "Have some patience, Cora. You're in Africa."

Cora looked at the nearly empty shelves. "I'm trying, but pretty soon we'll be eating mealies and peppermint candy morning, noon, and night. It's funny how things turned out."

"What d'ya mean?"

"Think about how much of a mission Bethel Methodist Church

would have had if the three of us hadn't volunteered." She rolled her eyes. "We are the mission, except for Reverend Pete. But he don't count because he's a professional missionary. What was he, a doctor before he came out here?"

"A nurse," Brenda replied.

"Well . . . either way, he's turned the village chief or medicine man or whatever he is into his assistant. Reverend Pete fills him with Christianity, and the Rain Chief turns around and pours it on the villagers."

Brenda stepped outside and Cora followed.

"That's what missionary work's all about." Brenda looked at her. "Have you seen Annette?"

"I think she's inside the church," Brenda said.

Cora walked down the dirt road that ran through the Zambian village. It was early, but already she could see waves of heat floating above the ground. Most of the villagers started their work before sunrise and had it wrapped up by noon. Annette always got up with them. Usually Brenda and Cora slept to a somewhat more decent hour.

Cora bathed quickly, using the half bar of soap with tender loving care. She dressed and headed for the tiny infirmary attached to the church. Thanks to Reverend Pete, the church with its stick cross was the sturdiest of all the buildings in the village. The villager's homes were more like permanent thatched-roof huts. They saw little need for anything more substantial.

As Cora crossed the road she saw Brenda preparing the outdoor school for the village children. She went in the church, walked through the room of worship and entered the sick room. There was no sign of Annette. This morning there were four patients in the space that was built to handle a total of six cots. Some kind of fever had hit the village and the Zambians were coming and going out of the infirmary like a revolving door. Whatever it was, for the villagers it wasn't very threatening. Two or three days of rest, distilled water, and the antibiotics supplied by the mission had them up and going in short order.

Cora liked working with the sick. No, what she really liked was the art of healing. To see a person, a plant, or an animal that was weak grow strong with health again: Cora found a sense of God in healing that she didn't find anywhere else.

Inside the infirmary, Cora made sure all the patients were comfortable, and assured them, with her limited *bemba* that breakfast would be served soon. Cora decided to check on the customary breakfast of mealies—maize cooked with water—after she took care of a much less attractive task. She had concluded there were aspects of being a missionary that were rewarding, but there were others that she could do without.

The makeshift commode, a hole with a strong, straight tree branch across it, was yards into the forest, but still Cora could smell the scent long before she reached it. Out of everything she had encountered as a missionary, this part of it ranked the lowest on her list. She held her breath as she approached the spot, but was stunned to see Annette lying with her head near the edge of the putrid orifice.

"Annette! What's wrong?" Cora rushed over and knelt beside her sister. The hot fetid air rushed into her lungs.

"All of a sudden I felt dizzy, and sick to my stomach." Annette's voice was weak, breathy. "I tried to make it back inside the village, but I couldn't."

"That's okay. It's okay, baby girl." Cora lifted Annette to her feet. Her dress was soaked with sweat. "Let me help you."

"I'm sorry," Annette apologized. "I must smell awful."

"Don't worry about that." Cora was shocked by the heat coming from Annette's body. "You're going to be okay." But because Annette could barely walk, it took them a good five minutes to make it back to the village.

"Don't take me to the infirmary," Annette whispered. "I want to go to our place."

"Whatever you want," Cora replied as Annette's eyes wavered. "We're almost there."

Winded, Cora lay Annette across the bed. "I'll be right back," she told her and ran out the door.

The schoolchildren were in the middle of singing "Jesus Loves Me" when Cora reached Brenda. "Where's Reverend Pete?" Her eyes searched the village.

"I think he's in the church. Why? Why are you looking like that?"

"Annette's sick. I think she's got the village fever." Cora looked at the ground but she couldn't hide the fear that was carved into her face. "She looks worse than any of the others I've seen."

"Where is she?"

"In our hut."

"Class is over for right now," Brenda announced. "I'll go to Annette. You find the Reverend."

Reverend Pete and Cora arrived at Annette's bedside in a matter of minutes. Brenda had taken off Annette's soiled clothes and was dressing her in a lightweight cotton gown.

The two sisters watched as the Reverend checked Annette's throat and eyes, took her temperature, and listened to her chest.

"She's got the same thing, all right. But it seems to be progressing faster, more aggressively, probably because she isn't a native." He looked at Cora and then Brenda. "I'm going to start her on the antibiotics, and we'll just have to keep a close watch over her and see how it goes. If we had a vehicle I'd just take her to the hospital." He looked down at Annette. "Now, I think our best bet is to do what we can. The supply truck should get here at any time. And if we need to, we can have them take Annette to the hospital in the city."

Reverend Pete opened his medical bag. The leather crackled because it was kept in the only refrigerator. He studied the contents and then he touched each bottle.

"What's wrong?" Cora asked. "Can't you find it?"

"There's a little here." He held up the near empty bottle.

"Is that all we have left?" Brenda's voice held alarm.

"I hate to say it, but it looks that way," Reverend Pete replied. "All our supplies are low, including the medicines."

Cora looked into Annette's frightened face. She knelt beside her and softly patted her head. "It's still going to be all right, baby girl. You just know that. The supply truck will be here at any moment."

Reverend Pete administered the antibiotic and left the room through a crowd of villagers who had gathered at the door. One of the barefoot children stepped inside, her eyes wide with concern. "Mis Ann-net sick?"

"Yes, she is." Brenda put her arm around the child's shoulders.

"I'll be fine," Annette said in a thin voice.

"See there," Brenda assured him. "So you all can go on. She needs to be alone so she can rest."

But Brenda and Cora's words did not prove to be true. Annette got sicker as the day turned into night and the supply truck did not arrive. They took turns sitting at her bedside, trying to keep her hydrated with water, although that was the only thing Annette would let pass her lips. Early the next morning she seemed to become more lucid, and Cora was glad to see a semblance of consciousness in her eyes.

"Cora," Annette whispered. "I want you to write a letter for me. I want you to write a letter to Michael and make sure he gets it."

"You just wait until you get better, Annette. I think that's the kind of letter you need to write yourself," she advised with a twinge of guilt.

"No. No. I want you to write it right now." She turned her head from side to side against the pillow. "I don't know if I'll get well and—"

"Don't say that." The words came out harsher than Cora wanted. "Don't you lie there and say that, Annie."

Annette just looked at her through clouded eyes.

"I'll write the letter for you if you really want me to, but I don't want to hear you say that again. Okay?" Cora fought the sting of tears.

Annette nodded, slowly.

Cora knew exactly where Annette kept her stationery and pens. She was the only one of them who had written back home consistently, most of the time including a sentence or two from her and

Brenda. Cora took up the pen and paper and sat down quietly, making sure she did not awaken Brenda. "Alright. I'm ready."

"I want . . ." Annette stopped speaking and swallowed. It appeared to be painful. Cora offered her more water, but she refused. "I want you to start it with 'Dearest Michael,' " Annette started her dictation.

"This is not the first time that I have written you since we have been in Africa." She spoke slowly. "But it is the first time that I am going to be bold enough to say the things that I believed a moral woman would never say to a man who is not her husband."

Cora's hand trembled as she placed the period behind the word *husband.*

"Since the very first day when you moved into the apartment above us, I have dreamed of being with you in every way a woman can be with a man. As you can see, my thoughts have not all been pure, but they were all based in love. If I never get the chance to tell you to your face—"

Cora put the pen down. "I'm not going to write this."

"Please," Annette beseeched her.

"I can't," Cora said, shaking her head.

"Ple-ease." The word had more strength than Annette appeared to have.

"Okay." Reluctantly, Cora picked up the pen again.

"I want you to know, I love you, Michael Dawson, and always will. Now," Annette rasped, "let me sign my name."

Cora watched as Annette signed it *Annie,* and then laid back as if it had taken more than she had. She took the letter and slipped it into the envelope. Afterwards Cora drifted into a troubled sleep.

Morning came and found Brenda and Cora awake. Annette was weaker than ever.

"I've got to do something," Brenda said. "I'm going to go up to the top of those rocks and see if I see the supply truck coming."

"All right," Cora replied. Despite a night of sleep Brenda's face looked drawn from worry.

Cora bathed Annette again, but this time she noticed a cool clamminess to her skin that had not been there before.

"I'm cold, Cora." The words were no more than a series of breaths.

Quickly, Cora took the sheets and covers from their beds and placed them all around Annette. "Is that better?"

"Yes," Annette said with effort. "But I believe I'm so cold because I'm afraid." Her weak eyes focused on Cora's face. "I'm afraid to die."

Cora started to shake her head.

"And I'm ashamed because I'm afraid. I should be happy because I'm going to see God." Annette closed her eyes and began to breathe through her mouth. "But instead I'm afraid."

Tears flowed down Cora's face as she leaned over her sister. "There's no need to feel ashamed, baby girl." Gently, Cora placed her hand on Annette's face. "You just concentrate on getting well." But Annette's eyes were closed, and she gave no response.

Cora turned toward the entrance to the hut when she heard footsteps. Brenda stepped inside. Her eyes were red. Her mouth trembled.

"You didn't see the truck?" Cora said.

Brenda nodded. "It's here."

"It's here?" Cora's voice rose. "Well, where is the medicine?"

"There isn't any." Brenda's voice quaked. "The refrigeration unit broke down and the antibiotic is no good."

"No good." Cora repeated the words as if she didn't understand.

"No," Brenda replied.

"No good," Cora repeated as she walked over to Brenda. "But we've got to be able to do something. We can't just let her die while she's on a mission for God," Cora cried.

"What can we do?" Tears spilled down Brenda's face.

"Maybe I can find some herbs that will help."

"What?" Brenda wiped her nose that had begun to run.

"There's got to be something like goldenseal or echinacea here." Cora brushed past Brenda. "Stay with her."

"Where are you going, Cora?"

"I don't know. But I can't stay here and do nothing. Just wait. I'll be back."

"Don't leave, Cora. She might—"

"I'll be back," she promised.

By the light of dawn Cora searched the nearby forest for any herbs that might save Annette. When the Rain Chief found Cora there was dirt in her hair, and her face was streaked with mud created by her tears.

Like a spirit he walked up to her. "You look for this?" The Rain Chief held out a plant.

Cora just stared.

"You look for this for Mis Ann-net."

Cora took the plant. She smelled it. "This will help Annette?"

"Yes," he said.

She looked at the plant, and then at the man with disbelief. "Why didn't you show it to us earlier?"

"Reverend Pete teach faith that God will heal. Pete have the medicine of God in the needle. This"—the Rain Chief shook the plant— "we use to heal the fever before we have the medicine of God."

Cora was dumbfounded. "You knew how to cure the fever with your own herbs but you never said anything because you thought it was against the Christian God?"

The Rain Chief simply looked at her.

She pushed herself off the ground. "We've got to get the medicine to Annette. We've got to hurry." Cora grabbed his arm. "Annette needs this. Reverend Pete doesn't have any more medicine."

When they reached the hut, there were villagers gathered outside. Cora pushed through the crowd, pulling the Rain Chief behind her. When she stepped inside the room she saw Brenda sitting in a chair. Her eyes were closed. Slowly, a sound erupted from Brenda's throat, a sound Cora had never heard before. Cora turned toward the bed where Annette lay. A sheet covered her entire body, including her face. Cora screamed so loud the jungle went silent.

Nebia's Story . . .

"Annette died?" Sheila asked. "Why did she have to die? She shook her head. "You could have made up something else for that part of the story, Miss Nebia." She sat back in her chair.

"But Annette did die," Nebia said softly. "This is a true story, and I must tell it as it happened."

Everyone was silent.

"When did it happen?" Cynthia asked.

"That was back in nineteen seventy-seven. Annette was nineteen years old."

"If she had lived we'd be the same age," Erica said softly. "I was still in college when Annette died." She paused. "So did they have a funeral and everything for her back here in St. Pete?"

"Yes they had a funeral. And everybody was there. Everybody except Cora."

Chapter 7

Laura's knees buckled when the first shovelful of dirt splattered against the top of the coffin. If it wasn't for Brenda and Nebia she would have fallen beside the gaping hole that held Annette's body in an ornate box. "I didn't want them to go no way," she moaned. "I didn't want them to go to Africa."

Brenda struggled with her mother's grief. "Come on, Mama. It's time to go home." Her eyes and her voice were full of tears. "Everyone is gone now."

"She's right, Miss Laura." Nebia spoke into Laura's ear as Laura leaned against her. "Annette is happy where she is now. You know in your heart that she'll always be with you. That we never really die," Nebia said as she strained under Laura's weight.

Laura took control of her body and nodded. She looked at the coffin one last time, and then turned away from the grave.

Michael fell in step behind them as they headed for his car. He was proud of the deuce and a quarter that he bought right after the Nova died, but Michael had never envisioned it as a funeral limousine.

Financially, things had begun to look up for Michael. His mother's only brother died and, since he was childless, what little he had he left to Michael. The inheritance was enough to convince the SBA that Michael would have a vested interest in his insurance company, and they approved his loan. With the money, he bought his licenses, permits, and bonds and opened a small space, Dawson Insurance.

Michael was the first to reach the Oldsmobile. He held the door open as he waited for Laura and Brenda to climb into the backseat. Nebia sat up front beside him. There would have been plenty of space for Cora who was lithe and limber, but Cora wasn't there.

On better days, full of chatter, they had all walked past the cemetery on their way home, but now no one spoke as Michael drove. The only sound was Nebia's low and mournful humming. Laura stared straight ahead, her life force weakened by the death of her youngest child. Brenda's eyes were downcast. Every so often she stole a glance at Michael's face through the rearview mirror. It took all of three minutes until they turned down the familiar narrow street, but it could have been three hours—and felt like much longer. Time, like reality, had been altered by Annette's passing.

The street was lined with cars, but a parking spot had been reserved for them directly in front of the Robinson home. Michael got out and opened the car doors. The last was Laura's. Michael stood and waited beside it, but Laura remained inside. She stared at the house she had lived in for fourteen years as if she had never seen it before.

"You come on out of there, Miss Laura," Nebia said as she placed her body between the two of them. "And I don't just mean out of that car." Nebia leaned inside the vehicle. "We need you here with us. We need all of you here."

Moments later Michael followed Nebia's lead. He moved back as Laura got out of the car. She touched Nebia's arm and smiled weakly at Michael and Brenda before she started up the walkway.

Inside the house Laura went upstairs and changed her shoes then threw herself into the heart of things. She seemed to draw energy from all the people and the activity. Laura made sure there wasn't a soul that she didn't speak to or who was without a plate of food.

"Don't you overdo it now, Mama," Brenda warned. Laura had gone off her diet while they were in Africa, and had gained a dangerous amount of weight.

"I'm fine, honey." Laura placed an apron around her midsection. "All of this will do me good. Keep my mind off of things." She dumped a pile of raw potatoes on the kitchen counter and began to peel them. Laura had bolted from paralysis to not being able to be still. Both reeked of instability.

Lucille came and stood beside Brenda. "Don't worry," Lucille said softly. "She'll be okay."

Brenda looked into Lucille's sad blue-grey eyes. Like her dyed ash-blond hair, they seemed so out of place in the sea of browns and blacks. At least that had not changed. It had been that way the entire time Lucille and Warren had lived in the all-black neighborhood. "I hope so," Brenda replied. She squeezed Lucille's hand.

Brenda walked into the crowded living room. She edged her way behind a row of occupied folding chairs that Michael had brought over from the community center the night before. Despite the somber occasion the room was filled with conversation and subdued snatches of laughter. Like a distant observer Brenda watched the scene. It was surreal. They had buried Annette no more than an hour ago, and now she had only one sister, Cora, and Cora was not there.

"Well, Miss Laura seems to be holding up pretty well, doesn't she?" A husky voice rose from beneath a fussy feather hat.

"Yes, chile. It seems that way, doesn't it? But you know she's got to be hurting something awful inside. Mm-mm-mm," another woman sitting in front of Brenda sounded.

"They'd just have to bury me with them if one of my children died before me." The feathers quaked as the woman spoke. "And they say Miss Laura and Annette hadn't really made up before the girls went traipsin' off to Africa. That had to make her death doubly hard."

"But gir-rl, what's even worse . . ." She leaned in so close one set of feathers mingled with the other. "Cora didn't come back for the funeral." The woman paused dramatically. "What's she doing over there in Africa? Some folks say she's grievin' so hard she couldn't come back. But I heard," she whispered, "she may have lost her mind."

"Now wouldn't that be something." The hat followed Laura's movements about the room. "Lawd, sometimes when it rains it pours."

Brenda wanted to put a stop to their gossiping, but the truth was she couldn't. She didn't know if Cora was crazy or sane, dead or alive. Nobody in St. Pete knew.

She looked out the window and saw Michael standing beside his car. Making more commotion than was necessary, Brenda made her way through the chairs and went outside to join him.

"So, how you doing?" he asked, his tone low.

"I guess I'm doing okay." Brenda crossed her arms in front of her. "It's just hard for me to accept this."

"Yes. It is very difficult," Michael replied.

They stood in silence before Brenda spoke again.

"I heard a couple of women in there"—Brenda motioned toward the house with her head—"talking about Cora."

It was the first time Brenda had spoken of Cora to Michael since she saw them embracing through the window of Michael's efficiency. Michael's eyes grew intense before he looked down. "What were they saying?"

"They were wondering why she stayed in Africa and didn't come back home."

"I can't say I hadn't wondered the same thing." Michael looked at Brenda again. "What did she say when you were about to come back?"

"She wouldn't say anything," Brenda replied. "She wouldn't talk to anybody. Cora wouldn't bathe and she wouldn't eat. There was nothing I could do to make her come back home with me."

"Damn." He covered his eyes. "Sounds like somebody needs to go over there and get her."

"Get her from where? Reverend Pete called this morning and said Cora was no longer in the village where we stayed. He doesn't know where she is."

"Damn," Michael repeated. He looked up the street.

"But Nebia says Cora's going to be alright," Brenda said softly.

"And how would she know that?" Michael swiped at a tear.

"She says that Yemaya, who's under God, has things for Cora to do right here on earth. That she'll protect her."

"Do you believe her?" Michael asked with guarded hope in his eyes.

"No." Brenda looked down. "I don't believe in that kind of stuff, but for Cora's sake I hope Nebia's right."

Michael put his hands in his pockets. "I'm not a believer either, but sometimes I hear different voices in Nebia's apartment when I know she's alone." He looked at Brenda. "And you and I both know Nebia's got a good command of her senses. And I don't think she was talking to herself." He paused. "Have you ever heard them?"

"No." Brenda looked skeptical.

"Well," Michael looked up the street again. "Voices or not, I hope Nebia's right."

Nebia's Story . . .

"So where was Cora?" Erica demanded.

"She was taken in by the widow of a leader of a small Bemba tribe. The woman's name was Chiti." Nebia nodded as she recalled. "Cora told me the only reason she survived Annette's death, the only reason her mind came back to her was because, in the beginning, she thought this Chiti was me." Nebia looked straight ahead. "But that girl stayed gone for months."

"Months?" Sheila repeated.

"This is some of the craziest stuff I ever heard," Cynthia declared. "It just don't seem real to me."

"It doesn't matter if it doesn't seem real to you or not." Nebia cut her eyes in Cynthia's direction. "It's what happened."

"So are you telling us the part about you talking to ghosts and spirits is true as well?" Sheila leaned forward. "I guess what I'm asking is, do you really talk to spirits?"

"This story isn't about me. It's about the Robinsons." Nebia searched the pocket of her shift. "But Yemaya did say that Cora was going to be alright. And at the time it was all we had to go on. To Laura, Brenda, and Michael it wasn't much, but it had to do." She lit a thin brown cigarette.

"I'ma tell you I've just about heard everything." Cynthia crossed her legs and eyed Nebia with disbelief.

"No. You haven't heard nothing yet." Nebia inhaled and blew a steady stream of white smoke into the clear night air.

Chapter 8

Brenda tapped on the door several times and waited. There was a rapid approach of footsteps before Michael opened the door.

"Hey. Come on in." He smiled before he walked back inside the efficiency. "I came back to get the rest of my stuff. You don't realize how much you have until you move." He motioned toward a pile in the middle of the floor. "I had no idea I had left all of this."

"I was wondering what was going on," Brenda said. "I heard someone walking around up here and I thought you were over at your new house."

"I was. As a matter of fact, I've been over there all morning." Michael faced Brenda. "The place really looks good now. You and Miss Laura got to come over and see it." He forced some of the articles from the pile into a garbage bag. "The carpenters finished up this morning. So it looks a lot different from when you last saw it. And it doesn't look anything like what Miss Laura saw before the work started."

"You sound like a proud father."

"I guess I am bragging." Michael gave an embarrassed smile.

"But it's okay." Brenda's eyes softened. "If I were moving into my own newly refurbished home, I'd brag too."

Michael smiled again. "So what are you up to today?"

"Nothing much," Brenda replied. "Mama, Nebia, and Lucille have gone to the Saturday flea market, so I was just laying around, looking at a little television. I'd love to go over to your house with you and see it."

"Sounds good to me." Michael's eyes sparkled. "It won't take me but a minute to finish up. Then we'll head on over there."

With Brenda's help it didn't take long for Michael to tie up the loose ends, and about thirty minutes later they were pulling up in front of Michael's new home. The freshly painted, two-story building stuck out like a new Saskatchewan dollar from the rundown houses around it. They were just as ornate, but their architectural beauty had been marred by time and neglect.

But that didn't bother Michael. "And this is just the beginning." He turned off the car as he continued to talk. "I believe there will come a time when most of these houses will be restored and Roser Park will be a historic neighborhood."

"You think so?" Brenda tried to visualize Michael's dream.

"I most certainly do." He put his arm on the top of the front seat behind her. "You see, I have plans here in St. Pete. I'm going to make my fortune and my mark, right here, even if it means opening up my own bank and loaning money to folks like us, who can't get loans anyplace else." He looked up and down the street. "Those kind of people will be able to get the money from me. Then they'll be able to buy a house in a neighborhood like this and help restore it." Michael looked at Brenda with determination. "Some kind of way it's going to happen."

"I'll bet you'll do just that," Brenda said, then added softly, "and I hope I'm around to share it."

"Of course you'll be around." Michael got out of the car. "Unless you plan on moving away from here."

Brenda joined him on the sidewalk in front of the house. "Nope." She continued with a sigh, "I don't plan to."

"Well, good. Things just wouldn't be the same if all of the Robinsons left St. Pete." His smile lightened his words, but still there was a remote sadness in Michael's eyes. "Come on. Let me show you inside."

Michael opened the door with pride. Inside the sunny, spacious rooms beamed, compliments of a repeated pattern of double windows with raised shades. Michael and Brenda's footsteps echoed along with their voices as they examined each one. Once in a while they came across a few choice pieces from Michael's old apartment.

"Is this the same light fixture that was in here the last time I came?" Brenda looked at an antique globe jutting out from the dining room ceiling.

"Sure is." Michael nodded. "It's amazing what a little water and bleach can do."

"Water, bleach, and paint." Brenda turned in slow circle. "This place looks wonderful. I could see the potential before but I had no idea it was going to look like this."

"Yeah." Michael took a deep breath. He looked from the formal dining room into the walk-in pantry inside the kitchen. "Now all I got to do is get some furniture. And get some paintings on the wall."

"Well, you've got a lot to do. You have a living room, dining room, library—" Brenda counted on her fingers.

"There are nine rooms in all, including the two bathrooms," Michael said.

"Babcock's is having a furniture sale this weekend. I saw it in the St. Pete *Times* this morning."

"Yeah?" Michael's interest rose.

"Uh-huh. And I'm pretty good at picking out furniture." She looked down. "Plus I love decorating. I could go with you, and give you my opinion, if you like."

Michael slid his hand into his jean pocket. "I don't want to take up all your time."

"You wouldn't be taking up all my time. I'd enjoy it," Brenda assured him. "Right now I can't think of anything better than shopping with somebody else's money."

"Oh, I see." Michael smiled. "Well, let's do it this way. If you help me pick out furniture and decorations, I'll cook you and Miss Laura dinner tonight as payment."

Brenda leaned back. "I didn't think you knew how to cook."

"Oh, I can cook. I just never had to while I was living in the efficiency," Michael replied. "Between Miss Laura and Nebia, somebody was always inviting me to eat or bringing me food." He folded his arms. "The truth is I can burn when I want to."

Brenda glanced at the ceiling, then back at Michael. "Sure you can."

"I can." He started to laugh.

"Well we shall see," Brenda challenged as they headed for the front door.

The next time Michael and Brenda entered the house it was hours later. Their timing for furniture shopping couldn't have been better. Michael bought a couple of rooms of furniture, and an eager Babcock Furniture Company delivered it. Now, the smell of spaghetti sauce blended with Michael's whistling as he busied himself in the kitchen. Brenda listened as she moved the last lamp for the last time. Her feet ached and, not being able to stand it any longer, she took her shoes off and stepped back to double-check her decision. Satisfied, Brenda sat down in one of the new dinette chairs. She grimaced as she pulled her foot onto her lap and squeezed. "I don't understand it."

"Understand what?"

"I don't understand how you have so much energy after shopping all day."

"And I don't understand how you can be so tired when everybody knows women are the champions of all shoppers," Michael replied.

"Yeah, but you and I have two different concepts of shopping. To me shopping means you browse and take your time. You enjoy the experience. You touch the fabric. Take in the colors." She sighed and sat back. "But evidently, to you shopping means rushing through the stores, writing down different styles and prices, and going back and choosing pieces through pure logic."

"My system doesn't sound too bad to me."

"It's not that it's bad," Brenda retorted. "It's just that you might have a heart attack from it."

Michael laughed.

"You can laugh, but I've never been in so many stores so quickly in all my life."

"I catch your drift." Michael poured the steaming pasta into a colander. "But considering everything, I think you did real good."

"Thank you." Brenda's voice changed ever so slightly. "We make quite a team, don't we?" She looked toward the kitchen longingly.

"Yep, we do," Michael threw over his shoulder. "But now your part of the bargain has been fulfilled. So all you've got to do is sit back and relax." He put the lid back on the pot. "It's too bad Miss Laura couldn't come. How's she doin'?"

"The bad days come and go," Brenda replied. "But she won't stick to the diet the doctor gave her. And whenever she eats something she's not suppose to, especially a lot of it, she doesn't feel well."

"I bet." Michael stirred the sauce. "Maybe she'll get accustomed to the diet after a while."

"Maybe," Brenda replied.

"Would you like to play some music?" he asked. "There's some tapes on top of the eight-track player."

"Sure." Brenda walked over and rifled through the small stack of tapes. Moments later the Isley Brothers began to croon "Living For The Love Of You."

"Turn it up. That's one of my favorites," Michael called.

"Mine too." Brenda tried to match his casual tone as she adjusted the volume. She closed her eyes and walked the room as she listened to the lyrics. When Brenda opened her eyes again, they focused on Michael as he stood in the kitchen with his back turned. She walked toward him.

"The food will be ready in about five minutes," Michael said as he turned, only to find Brenda standing a few feet away. "Oh. I didn't realize you were in here."

"I just came in." Brenda stepped a little closer.

"Would you care for something to drink? Some wine?"

"Are you drinking?" Brenda looked into his eyes.

"Nope. But don't let that stop you."

She looked down. "A woman doesn't want to drink alone, Michael."

"If you say so." He made a funny face. " The crazy games women play. But you know, between me and you, if you want a drink, all you have to do is say so."

"And why is it so simple between us?" The question was soft and quiet.

"Because . . ." Michael shrugged.

"Because we don't have that kind of relationship?"

"That's right," he replied.

A pensive smile lit Brenda's face. She leaned against the refrigerator. "We've known each other for quite a while, haven't we?" Brenda continued with another question before Michael could answer. "Do you remember the night Annette introduced us?"

Michael nodded. "Sure I do. It seems like yesterday but it was couple of years ago. And it's been a while since Annette . . . has been gone."

"Yes." Brenda looked down at her hands. "I miss her."

"We all do," Michael said softly.

Brenda lifted her chin. "When Annette introduced us that day . . . my heart was beating so hard I thought it was going to burst right through my chest."

"Really?" Michael stopped stirring and looked at her.

"I remember asking you if you ever attended A&M," Brenda continued. "But I already knew the answer, because from the very first time I saw you I had feelings for you." She looked at Michael with full eyes. "But there you were, being introduced to me by my little sister as the man of her dreams."

"Brenda . . . wait." Michael touched her shoulder.

"No," she said. "I need to say this."

Michael shook his head.

"You don't want to hear it," she continued softly. "But I've got to say this, Michael. I've held back for so long. If Annette were still here, these words would never pass my lips. You would never know how much I care for you. But she's gone, Michael, and I know Annette would want the best for you. And the best for me." Brenda's hand went to her heart. "I can make a good home for you, Michael. We could be so good together. And you couldn't find a better business partner anywhere in St. Petersburg."

"Brenda. Please . . . stop." His hand tightened on her arm.

"Won't you give us a chance?" Brenda implored. "Won't you give me a chance to make you happy? To turn this house into a home." Her words hung in the air.

"Brenda." Her name broke the silence. "You're an attractive woman, and one day the right man will come along." Michael had to look away before he continued. "But that man is not me. It's not me, Brenda."

"You could learn to love me," she softly insisted.

"For a man like me, that would leave the door wide open for trouble. And that wouldn't be fair to you or me," Michael replied.

"I see."

There was an awkward silence.

"I see." At first Brenda covered her mouth with a shaky hand. Then she tried to smile and cover the hurt. Finally, Brenda looked at the stove. "I think the sauce is ready. You better pour it over the spaghetti before it starts to stick. I'll set the table."

Hesitantly, Michael turned back to the stove as Brenda removed two plates from a cardboard box. She walked to the dining room and put the plates on the table. The sound the ceramic dishes made when they met the wood table seemed inordinately loud. But the sound of Brenda closing the front door behind her without saying good-bye was even louder.

Michael turned and stared in the direction of the living room.

Afterwards he held on to the rim of the kitchen sink and hung his head.

Nebia's Story . . .

"Oh my God." Sheila held her fingers to her mouth. "I couldn't have stayed after that either. Talk about rejection."

"I couldn't have said that stuff in the first place," Erica remarked. "I mean, really. Annette had been in love with him. I think Michael nipping it in the bud served Brenda right."

"All I've got to say is, right or wrong," Nebia said, "Michael did turn her down. Of course he was only trying to be true to his own feelings. And you have to realize they were all feeling Annette's death mighty heavily." Nebia looked into all three of their faces. "People make all kinds of strange choices when loved ones die, almost as if reality is so shaky they lose their own true selves . . . or else they find them." Nebia released her next words with a heavy breath. "I don't know which one it was in Cora's case."

"Cora came back?" Cynthia asked.

"Ye-es. Cora came back just like a hurricane. You knew that she had arrived, but you didn't know what the consequences were gonna be."

Chapter 9

"How you doin', Miss Laura? Miss Nebia?" Michael asked as he stood on the stairs of the Robinsons' apartment building. "I was driving by and I saw you sitting out here. I thought I'd come up and say hello."

"You bet' not see us out here and pass by without stopping," Laura replied. But Nebia got up and went to the furthest corner of the front porch. Laura followed her movements with a frustrated glare. "Don't you know how to speak, woman?"

Nebia put up her hand to shush her.

Laura gave her a chastised look. "Next time, Michael, you know not to ask after her."

"It doesn't matter." Michael glanced at Nebia. "I know Miss Nebia doesn't mean any harm."

"Well." Laura nodded. "I'm glad you see it that way." She smiled as a distant thumping began. "But I tell you, I've been doing pretty good, myself." Laura leaned forward in her chair as a couple of children on bicycles stopped riding to look back. "What is that noise?"

"I don't know." Michael took his foot off the stairs and started back up the walkway. "There's a crowd of people coming down the street." He shielded his eyes from the sun. "It sounds like a drum to me."

"It's Cora," Nebia said in a powerful whisper.

The metal hinges of the screened door creaked as Brenda came out onto the porch. She stood by her mother's chair as the drumming strengthened along with a faint voice that wove in and out of the beats.

"Cora?" Laura said her daughter's name as she heaved her body out of the chair. "That's Cora's voice." She wrapped her arm around one of the porch columns.

By now Cora's voice filled the street. The words were foreign, but the tone was as solemn as any funeral.

"It is Cora," Laura repeated as she and Brenda walked down the stairs and joined Michael on the sidewalk. Michael glanced at Brenda, but she continued to look straight ahead.

By then they could see Cora's gold wrap billow around her like a vibrant aura as she drummed and sang. Some of the children ran up and joined her, oblivious to the tears that coursed down Cora's face. They did not recognize the pain in Cora's song, so they moved with the drumbeat in comical fashions. Then one after the other they saw her face and stopped their antics, but they continued to walk with her, their eyes wide with questions. By then Cora's tears had nearly stopped, but as she neared the house she grew up in, a new downpour began.

Laura cried too as she stood on the public sidewalk with Brenda, Nebia, and Michael a few feet behind. When Cora reached her mother she placed the drum on the ground and took hold of Laura's hands. "The people I stayed with say the vibration of the human voice goes on forever. So I sang from Annette's grave to our house. That way she will always know where home is no matter where she died. It's the only gift I could give Annette and you, Mama, after being gone for so long."

"Thank you, baby. There's no way Annette will forget now." Laura threw her arms around her daughter. "Been gone? Time means nothing now that I'm holding you in my arms. Welcome home,

Cora." Laura's ivy arms clung to her daughter as tears spilled down both their faces.

Cora closed her eyes as Laura's motherly love washed over her. She opened them and looked straight into Brenda's eyes. For a moment their gazes held before Cora gently moved away from Laura and over to her sister.

"Brenda . . ." She searched the eyes that were so much like her own.

There was only a split second when their arms didn't know what to do, but then they hugged.

"Welcome home, Cora. It's good to see you," Brenda said.

"It means so much to hear you say that," Cora replied.

They shared a final squeeze before Cora stepped away. She looked at Michael. "So you're still here." Her lips held a slight, warm smile.

"Where else would I be? I've made St. Petersburg my home." He stammered as a light entered his eyes.

She rose on her toes and gave him a peck on the cheek. "Yes. Where else?"

"It's good to see you, Cora," Michael said, his voice full.

"You too," she replied. "All of you." Cora added almost too quickly as she looked from Brenda to her mother, and finally at Nebia, who remained at the top of the stairs.

Cora ran to meet Nebia. "Nebia . . . Nebia, I've thought of you so often." She grabbed her hand.

"I have thought of you, too." Her steely gaze bore into Cora's wet eyes. "And because of that we were never parted."

Cora shook her head as tears mingled with laughter. "Never." She turned back toward the street; she looked at her family, friends, and neighbors, at old faces as well as new ones. "It's good to be back," Cora announced.

Laura took a few quick but stiff steps toward the house. "Are you hungry?"

"I could eat," Cora said.

Laura stepped onto the first step and then the next. "Well, I better get in here and fix you something." Cora grabbed her arm. "Something that you really like. Just name it." She beamed. "And mama is sure to please."

"I could do with some of your good vegetables and . . . some cornbread."

"Vegetables and cornbread." Laura leaned back. She looked Cora up and down. "Looks like you need a little meat on your bones to me."

"I'm sure that's what you think," Cora said. "But I feel good and the truth is I don't eat that much meat anymore."

"My stars." Laura opened the screen door and stepped inside the house. "We gon' have to fix that."

Nebia's Story . . .

"She came back," Erica exclaimed. "How long was Cora gone?"

"A year, three months, and five days," Nebia replied without hesitation.

"You remember it so well," Cynthia said. "Miss Laura had to be happy, too."

"And Brenda," Sheila added.

"Yes. Brenda too," Cynthia agreed.

"Mm-hmm," Nebia sounded. "We were all deeply moved that Cora had returned to us. Especially Michael. A glow came over his face when he saw her. I told you I watched it all from the porch. I saw every one of their faces. Laura's joy. Brenda's uneasy happiness. And Michael's surrender to Cora."

"Do you think Brenda saw that?" Erica asked.

Nebia leaned toward her. "I don't know if she saw it that day, but it wasn't long before everybody knew."

Chapter 10

Miss Laura sighed as she wiped her hands on her apron. "It almost seems like old times again. Almost." Her smile was forlorn before her chest lifted. "Although I miss my Annette, it surely feels good having you back." She looked at Cora, who smiled.

"And a great meal like the one we just had only adds to the pleasure," Michael said as he stood up.

"It was good, wasn't it?" Miss Laura's smile broadened.

"Mighty good, Mama," Cora said. Brenda simply nodded.

Laura used the arm of the couch as a counterweight to push her way onto her feet. "It doesn't hurt seeing you around here so often either, Michael. For a while there I thought you had forgotten us."

Michael glanced at Cora before he looked at Miss Laura. "There is no way I could ever forget you, Miss Laura. You know that."

"Either way," Laura replied, "it's good. It's all good."

Michael pushed the chair up to the table. "I guess I ought to be going. I don't want to wear out my welcome."

"I've got to go, too," Brenda said. "They've asked me to head up a community organization. So I've got a meeting to go to."

"What kind of organization?" Cora asked.

"It's just getting started," Brenda replied. "But it's a neighborhood watch program. We've had quite a few problems lately with the young boys out here trying to prove they're men with knives and guns. I'm organizing a group that will help our neighbors feel a little safer."

"Sounds good." Cora smiled at her sister.

"And you'll be just the person to do it, too," Michael added.

Brenda looked at him, then looked away.

"Where's it going to be held? At the community center?" Michael tried to engage her.

"No. No." Brenda looked him. "It's going to be at Rising Star Baptist Church. The church is thinking about backing me on this. They've got a community outreach program and they want me to consider starting a tutoring program for the youth."

"Seems like a match," Cora said as Miss Laura crossed her arms.

"You sound rather interested, Cora. Do you want to come?"

Cora shook her head. "No-o. It's not for me." She tried to soften her reply. "But I can see you doing it. Me . . . I'm thinking about going right on down to the beach. I want a little quiet time with nature."

"Brenda just told you how dangerous it's gotten around here, Cora," Miss Laura warned. "I don't know if it's wise for you to go down there and be sitting on that beach in the dark by yourself."

"I'll be fine, Mama. Believe me," Cora assured her. "Over this past year I've dealt with more than young thugs who think that violence is a way to show their strength." Cora rose from her chair. "But you're right about it getting dark. So I'm going to leave right now. I won't be too long." She walked toward the front door. "Good night, Michael. And I'll see you later, Brenda." Cora opened the door and closed it behind her.

Moments later Brenda and Michael got into their cars and drove off. But as Michael got further down the street the headlights of his Olds 225 caught Cora in their glare. He rolled down the window and began to drive beside her.

"Perhaps Miss Laura was right, Cora. It is kind of dark out here for you to be walking to that beach alone. Would you care for some company?"

"Are you into nature?" Cora continued to walk as Michael's car crept beside her.

"Can't say I have been, but I can sit quietly and wait while you do what you need to do. I don't mind."

Cora stopped and Michael stopped his car. "Michael, I just . . ." She drew a deep breath.

"What is it, Cora? You've been acting as if I bite or something." There was a stare-down. "I'm the same Michael you used to know. No different. No different at all."

Cora smiled into his honest, open eyes. "I know you don't bite. And sure"—she shrugged—"you can take me to the beach." She walked around the car and climbed in on the passenger's side.

It was a short ride filled by a few idle words, shadowed by unspoken thoughts. When Cora and Michael climbed out of the car it was almost dark. It grew darker still as they walked onto the beach, away from the lit parking lot. Without ceremony Cora sat on the sand. Hesitantly, Michael looked around him before he joined her a few feet away.

"The Mother feels so good." Cora ran her hands over the ground.

"She does?" Michael asked.

"Yes. Yes, she does. If you just try"—Cora closed her eyes—"you can feel it too. You'll feel it in your heart. While I was in Zambia there was nothing that fed me more than going out and sitting near the Zambezi River. It was amazing because the water was so alive there. I knew it was alive. I knew its moods by the sounds it made."

"I've never thought about water being alive. Or having moods." Michael shook his head. "It just never occurred to me. To be honest with you, I just don't understand."

Cora reached out toward the water. "It's got to be alive, Michael. How can it not be? We are. And the same thing that created us, created it." She paused. "The Tonga tribe that I lived with were forced to leave the banks of the Zambezi back in the 50's. I stayed with a Tongan woman named Chiti. She was a widow and a medicine woman. The entire village would give her food because she had no man to take care of her. But it was also because she was an asset to the village. She had knowledge of herbs and spirits . . ." Cora glanced at Michael. ". . . and human nature. So they fed her, and in the very beginning when things were very rough for me, she made sure I ate too." Cora knocked the sand from her hands. "From time to time Chiti and I would leave the barren highlands and go to a place near the banks of the Zambezi. There we would stay for a week at a time eating from the land and drinking of the spirit of the earth."

"My God, Cora. Only you would be able to do something like that." Admiration filled Michael's words. "I think of Africa with dangerous animals and a tough life, but there you were living it."

"I did what I had to do at the time, Michael. I couldn't come back here. I couldn't come back." She shook her head. "And there was danger. I nearly lost my mind after Annette's death. If it hadn't been for Chiti, I don't know what would have happened to me. But she brought me back from the brink and kept me alive during the process. Yes." She looked at him. "There were times I was frightened of the animals, but there were other times when they were so beautiful. I've seen elephants, and giraffes and antelopes, and warthogs, spotted hyenas, and even leopards. And from sandpipers to babblers. I've seen some of everything, Michael, but nothing was nearly as frightening as being lost in the abyss of my mind, and the guilt around Annette."

"I guess we've all dealt with guilt, but what can we do?" Michael asked. "We can't change the past. We've got to live for right now and hope that any mistakes we may have made, that we won't repeat them. At least that's how I've managed to go on."

"Yes." Cora sighed. "There is only right now." She placed her hands firmly on the ground beside her. "And right now I just want to sit here."

Michael got quiet as Cora drew into herself. He waited and watched her silhouette against the night. Her locked hair was majestic, a mighty crown on her head, and finally, after an indeterminable amount of time, Michael heard Cora softly say, "I'm glad to be back, Michael, but somehow I . . . I don't know." She shook her head. "I've lost the feeling of belonging."

"Give yourself a little more time, Cora. You've only been home now for two weeks. It's going to take time."

"Maybe," Cora replied. "But it might be just that I've changed so much that . . . or that we lost so much . . ." Cora looked down.

"Let's not talk about it." Michael moved closer to her. "It's not going to do any good to talk about it."

"But what can we do? What?" Even in the dark he could see the plea in her eyes.

Michael put his arm around Cora's shoulders.

"If a year away from the place that I was born, a place that held so many memories that I couldn't stand coming back, didn't do any good, what will?" Cora trembled.

"You're cold," Michael said.

"No," Cora replied. "At least not on the outside."

He placed both arms around her. Cora leaned against him. "What a life, Michael. What a life."

"Yes. But we've got to live it." He rubbed his face against her hair.

Cora faced him. "But how can we?" The question addressed more than what had been discussed.

"How can we not?" Michael and Cora's eyes locked before he kissed her.

At first Cora kissed him back, but then she turned her head. "I haven't had a man in a long time. If we go further than this, I don't want you to think it means—"

"I'll accept it just for what it is," Michael cut her off. "I won't expect more than you can give me, Cora."

She weighed what he said. "I hope not." Cora initiated the second kiss, and then they loved each other on the sand.

After Michael dropped her off, Cora entered the house quietly. She didn't want to wake her mother or Brenda. She walked to the downstairs bathroom and flipped on the light. Cora turned to close the door, but Brenda was standing in the hall.

"I thought I heard a car door slam out front. It was getting late and I was concerned about you."

"Yeah, it's me." Cora looked in Brenda's eyes. "Michael dropped me off. He ended up going to the beach with me."

"Oh." Brenda's eyes roamed over Cora's hair. It was full of sand. "I see."

Cora shook her locks. Sand trickled to the floor.

They stood in silence before Cora said, "Thanks for thinking about me. Sleep well."

"I hope you can do the same." Brenda walked away.

Nebia's Story . . .

"Busted," Cynthia said. "Totally busted."

"Yes, she was," Erica replied. She shook her head. "How in the world did they sleep together? Cora had only been home for two weeks."

"But she'd been gone for nearly a year." Sheila defended Cora.

"So what's that mean?" Erica asked. "That it's okay to have sex with the guy your sister was in love with because a year had passed?"

"You didn't say anything negative about Brenda when she was trying to get it on with Michael."

Erica raised her shoulders. "That was different. Brenda wanted to build a life with him and have a family and—"

"And all that respectable stuff," Cynthia replied. "See, that's why you defended Brenda." Cynthia made a face. "But it's about the same thing."

"No it's not." Erica dug in.

"I think either way, this is going to be nothing but a mess," Sheila said.

"It didn't end up being pretty," Nebia replied. "Not pretty at all."

"So what happened? Did Cora and Michael just sneak around

and sleep together, trying to hide it from everybody?" Erica crossed her arms.

"No, no." Nebia shook her head adamantly. "You really have Michael wrong. It wasn't his intention to disrespect the Robinsons. He was a man with a good heart, a weak one"—she squinted—"but good. And it seemed the Robinsons could turn his heart on a dime."

Chapter 11

Brenda forced the garbage down into the garbage can and turned back toward the house. She stopped and looked at the upper loft of their dilapidated garage. Cora had converted the uninhabitable space into a makeshift art studio.

"Cora." Brenda mounted the rickety stairs. "Cora? You up here?"

"Yeah."

"Didn't you hear us calling you a little while ago?"

"Not really." Cora dabbed more paint onto the canvas. She stepped back and examined her painting.

"Michael was here looking for you. We called back here. I don't know how you didn't hear us." Brenda's face hardened. "When you didn't answer, we told Michael you weren't here."

"Oh." Cora glanced at Brenda then she refocused on the canvas.

Brenda walked over and stood beside the painting. "What is that, Cora?"

"It's baskets. A group of Plateau Tonga baskets. The women in Zambia would weave them out of palms. Malala palm leaves."

Brenda studied the collage of baskets with striking patterns that resembled woven diamonds within diamonds. "I'm not talking about

the baskets. What's that thing behind them? It looks like a figure."
Brenda skimmed over Cora's small collection of paintings. "See,
there it is again." She pointed. "It seems to be in everything you
paint."

Cora put her brush down. "I guess it's . . ." She hesitated. "It's
Annette's spirit. I feel like Annette's spirit is always with me. No
matter what I do she comes through in my paintings. The Tonga
believe that when a person dies, their spirit desires a relationship
with one of the living family members." She focused on Brenda.
"Sometimes it's done through jewelry, beadwork or something
that the person wore, and the family member, the one the spirit is
connected to, would have that as an heirloom." Cora paused. "I
don't know how else to explain it. The image always seems to come
from my hands before I even know I've painted it."

"So you believe it's Annette," Brenda said, her shoulders stiff.
"That Annette is with you."

"Yes." Cora stared at the newest painting. "That's the only thing
that makes sense to me."

"Why you, Cora? Are you so special that it would be *you* that
Annette would want to remain in contact with?"

"No." Cora's brow lowered. "I don't believe it has anything to do
with that. I believe it may have to do with my being more open to
the spirit world."

Brenda looked down, then up again. "So you believe Annette is
with you. Then that would mean she's aware of everything you're
doing now."

Their eyes locked.

"Yes, that would be right," Cora replied.

"So Annette knows about Michael and you?"

Cora turned her back and dipped her brush in a cleaning solu-
tion. "Brenda, I don't think you and I need to talk about this. There's
just too many feelings around this for you."

"Too many feelings around this for me?" Brenda repeated. Then
her eyes narrowed. "Yes, there is. But it's not just because Michael
was Annette's first love, I couldn't be so hypocritical as to say that,

but what bothers me, Cora, is . . . I don't believe you really love him. I truly don't. I don't know if you are capable of loving any man . . . anybody."

Cora kept her back turned as Brenda continued.

"You heard us calling you, Cora, but you ignored us. You knew Michael was here and you simply ignored us."

"Brenda, I said I don't want to talk about this."

"Do you love him, Cora? Do you really love him?"

Cora looked at Brenda. "Of course I love Michael."

Brenda looked disgusted. "Of course, you do."

Cora inhaled. "Michael doesn't need you to defend him. Believe me, he doesn't. And your defending him and trying to protect him from me is only because of how you truly feel about him."

Brenda's chin lifted. "Yes. I do care for Michael. I want the best for him. He's a good man. He deserves a woman who will be in his corner, help him with his business, his home. He deserves all of that, Cora. Can you give that to him? Are you willing to?"

Cora's voice softened. "I never promised Michael anything."

"I'm sure you haven't," Brenda replied. "When have you ever promised somebody something, Cora, besides something that serves you? Can you remember?"

Cora stared at the shadowy form on the fresh painting.

"It probably was so long ago, we were still children. I know it was before you became this woman who just uses the world to her advantage. No matter how it hurts others." Brenda shook her head. "Not one day have you gone out and looked for a job since you've been here. And that savings account that you started a long time ago hasn't benefited anybody but you. Are we suppose to take care of you, Cora? Do Mama and I owe you that?"

There was a pause before Cora spoke with resignation. "It's not my intention to use or hurt anyone."

"Only God can appreciate your . . . intent, Cora. We regular human beings down here need action. Pure dee action." Brenda walked out.

After Brenda left, Cora stared at the canvas in front of her before she dropped to the dirty floor. She looked through tears at the ghostly image that loomed behind the baskets, between the pottery, and above the beaded necklaces. "Annette. Annette," she repeated in a whisper. "Annette. Why didn't they take me instead of you?"

Nebia's Story . . .

"Man, they were both hurting, and it must be re-eally hard when you and your sister are going through something like that," Cynthia remarked.

"Yeah." Sheila nodded.

"I don't know how they're going to work it out," Cynthia continued. "Cora seems like she's in such a space that she's not able to do more than what's she's doing."

"I don't know if she really wants to." Erica looked unconvinced.

"Why do you say that?" Cynthia asked.

"She just seems to be so locked within herself." Erica touched her heart. "You've got to think about the other person."

"And you aren't the only person who felt that way," Miss Nebia joined in. "Brenda did, too. It frustrated her to no end that Cora couldn't seem to see beyond her own turmoil."

"So what did they end up doing?" Sheila asked.

"Well." Nebia pulled the loose skin on her throat. "Cora did what she did best."

Chapter 12

"I don't want you to ride to the airport with me, Mama." Cora looked into Laura's eyes. "That's money you can keep in your pocket. These cab rides aren't free, you know."

"I know that," Laura said. "But it should be my choice."

"No. It should be my choice," Cora said. "I thought we said our good-byes early this morning. You were supposed to be with Nebia. What are you doing back home?"

"I couldn't stay away, Cora. I had to be here." Laura pleaded for understanding.

Cora put her arms around her mother. "I do understand." She held tight. "And I hope you understand that I just can't stay any longer. I've got to go back."

"Why? Why? Aren't we enough for you here?" Laura shut her eyes. "Isn't this enough?"

Cora leaned back and looked deep into her mother's face. "It has nothing to do with you. You've got to believe that, Mama. Brenda and Nebia have accepted it. Why can't you?"

Because they're not your mama. I am." Tears spilled down Laura's cheeks.

Cora hugged her again.

"Ma'am," the cab driver called. "I hope you know this meter is ticking in here."

"Yes. Yes," Cora spoke toward the open cab window. "I'm coming."

"How long you goin' to be gone this time?" Laura wiped her nose.

"I don't know." Cora looked uncomfortable. "I just know I have to go. It's like something there is calling me."

"And what about Michael?"

Cora looked down. "Right from the beginning I told him not to expect much from me. I told him I would only give him what I could. I hope that he will understand."

Laura's eyes widened. "You hope he'll understand. Didn't you tell him?"

Cora shook her head. "I couldn't." This time it was Cora's eyes that pleaded. "I couldn't tell him."

"Oh, Cora." Laura shuddered.

"I know I'm so selfish." She shut her eyes. "I've never been any good, Mama. You've got to face that fact."

Laura squeezed Cora's arm. "I won't hear such a thing out of you. I don't ever want to hear you say that. You are good, Cora. You are good deep inside. You can't be but what you are. A wild thing. And we all got to understand that. Michael included." Laura stroked Cora's arm. "So you remember that while you're over there in Africa. You remember that no matter what happens, Cora Robinson. My girl. My sweet girl." She touched Cora's face. "You remember Cora is a good woman. She always has been. She always will be."

"Ma'am," the cab driver warned.

"I'm coming." Cora gave her mother one last squeeze. "I'll see you, Mama."

"Yes. We'll see each other soon," Laura said with confidence, but her face trembled as she held back tears.

Cora climbed into the backseat of the cab. Laura shut the car door and leaned over. "See you soon, Cora."

"Yes, Mama. Good-bye." Cora blew a kiss as the car pulled off. "Good-bye, baby." Laura waved.

Laura continued to wave until the taxi was no bigger than one of her tears.

Later that afternoon while Laura baked biscuits, the doorbell rang. "Just a minute," she called. Laura eased out of the chair and made her way to the front door. She opened it and there stood Michael. "Hello," she said.

"Good afternoon, Miss Laura. I guess you are surprised to see me."

"I sure am." She unlatched the screen door. Laura hesitated a split second. "Come on in."

"Thanks. I'm not going to stay long, Miss Laura." Michael held the screen door so it wouldn't slam. "But I knew this was the time of day that Cora normally takes her walk and I just wanted to show you something before I gave it to Cora."

"What is it?" Laura stopped in the middle of the floor.

Michael smiled. "I've got something for Cora and I want you to see it first. I want to know what you think about it, because I know you know what she likes."

"Michael wait, I—"

"No-no. I want to show it to you." He pulled a velvet box out of his pocket and opened it. A small diamond ring gleamed inside. "I'm going to ask her to marry me, Miss Laura." Michael looked at Cora's mother. "I'm going to ask her tonight." He tried to give her the box. "Do you think she'll like it?"

"Oh, no," Laura moaned.

"You don't think so." Michael looked at the ring.

"No, you misunderstood me. Of course Cora would like it, Michael. Any woman would."

He exhaled. "Good. You had me scared there for a minute." A smile took over his face.

Laura heaved a sigh. "Michael . . . I've got something to tell you."

"What is it, Miss Laura? Is something wrong with Cora?"

"No-no. Nothing's wrong with her, Michael. At least nothing that we can do anything about."

"What do you mean?"

Laura looked down. "Michael . . . Cora's gone back to Africa."

"Gone back to Africa?" He stared at her as if he didn't understand.

"Yes. She left this morning."

"But I was just with Cora last night."

Laura looked down.

"She couldn't have left. Is this a joke?"

"No, Michael." Laura touched his arm. "I wish it was. She left a couple of hours ago."

"But why?"

"I asked her why." Laura shook her head. " She said she just had to go. She felt like Africa was calling her. And you know Cora."

"But I didn't tell her . . . she-she didn't know I was going to give her this." Michael stammered. "Maybe if she had known." His eyes took on a wild look. "Maybe I can still tell her. What time is her flight?"

"It leaves in about—" Laura looked at the clock on the wall. "It leaves in about twenty-five minutes."

"Then maybe I can stop her and make her understand."

"Michael." Laura's eyes went sad. "I don't th—"

"No! Cora just didn't understand. She didn't know that I wanted to marry her. That this wasn't just some kind of thing for me. If she had known that I know she wouldn't have left." He pleaded for his words to be true. "She wouldn't have left me, Miss Laura. So I've got to tell her." Michael backed toward the door. "I can get to the airport before she leaves."

"Michael! Please!"

"No. I've got to try." He opened the screen door. "I've got to try." It slammed behind him.

Michael rushed down the stairs and jumped into his car. Laura held the door open and watched him speed off just as Brenda drove up and parked.

She climbed out of the car and looked up the street as Michael's car disappeared. "What happened? He's going to get a ticket driving like that."

"I hope he doesn't." Laura pressed her hand against her face. "The boy don't need no more worries."

"Where is he going driving like that?" Brenda walked toward the stairs.

"He's trying to catch Cora before her plane takes off." Laura heaved a sigh. "He was going to ask her to marry him today."

Brenda's mouth hardened. "This is awful. And Cora probably knew it was coming and that's why she left. If she wasn't my sister, Mama, I'd say—"

"Don't speak ill of Cora," Laura demanded. "Nobody knows her pain but her. Don't speak ill of your sister."

"And this is how it's always been." Brenda crossed her arms. "Cora and Cora's pain. What about other people, Mama? When is Cora going to care about other people?" Brenda slammed the screen door.

Michael drove faster and faster. Suddenly, he whizzed through a stop sign and barely missed an oncoming car before he pulled over to a curb. Michael hung his head. "Cora, you didn't have to go. We love you here. I love you."

He leaned back against the car seat and closed his eyes.

Nebia's Story . . .

"How long was she in Africa this time?" Cynthia asked.

"Nine months," Nebia replied.

"Miss Nebia, didn't you think it was rather selfish for Cora to leave like that?" Sheila asked. "I mean, she just up and left everybody, and she didn't even tell Michael."

"That was Cora. When I look back on it now, I would say Cora was a little bit of everything. Goodness. Sweetness. Bitterness. Cruelty. But what it all amounted to in my eyes was someone who was being herself. You never could say Cora wasn't that."

"So what does that mean?" Erica retorted. "We're all suppose to do what ever the heck we please, no matter what harm it does?"

"No," Nebia replied quietly. "No, I wouldn't say that's the way to live. I'm simply telling you that's the way Cora lived her life. And I respected her for that even though I didn't always agree with how she lived it."

"Poor Laura," Sheila said. "It's obvious Cora had a special place in her heart, but she just kept breaking it by leaving. I don't know how she ever forgave her for that."

Nebia rocked back and forth. "Believe me, she did. And the truth is, Laura never abandoned Cora. But I can't say she was the same with everyone."

Chapter 13

"I didn't say a word when you picked up that first package of ginger snap cookies." Brenda crossed her arms in the grocery store. "But now you've got another one. Mama, you know good and well that—"

"Leave me alone," Laura replied and put the second package of cookies in the cart. "Let them tell it, I can't enjoy anything anymore." She moved slowly down the aisle. "So I don't care what that doctor says. I'm going to have something good in my life."

"All right." Brenda turned her head. "I'm not going to say anything else."

Laura huffed. "Do you promise?"

"What are you two talking about?"

Laura leaned on the basket for support as she turned around. "Michael. I knew it was you. I didn't have to see your face. I know your voice."

"How you doin', Miss Laura?"

"I'm just fine. Glad to see you. You're lookin' good."

"The same goes for you."

Laura rolled her eyes. "You're just lying now. But I appreciate it anyway."

"Hi, Michael," Brenda said with a kind of sweetness.

"Hey. How you doin'?"

"I'm good."

"That's great," Michael replied.

"How's life been treating you?" Laura asked.

"I can't complain. Business has picked up and I've got my own little storefront agency down on Ninth South. So what can I say?" He smiled and nodded. "Life has been treating me pretty fairly."

"I meant to tell you I saw your name on a list of businesses that we plan to ask to help support Community Ties," Brenda said.

"Oh-h." Both of Michael's eyebrows rose.

"And we don't hit up anybody but the businesses we think are doing pretty well." She smiled.

Michael smiled too. "Tell me anything."

"Oh no." Brenda's voice softened. "You're really doing great, Michael. I'm proud of you."

Laura's eyes narrowed as she watched Brenda.

"I hoped I'd see you at some more of the meetings." Brenda looked down almost as if to compose herself. "You came to a couple of them and then you stopped."

"I've been working in the evenings," Michael replied. "But I'll be back."

"Really? I'd love to see you, Michael."

Michael gazed at Brenda. "It's a done deal."

"Or better still," Brenda chimed, "I can bring the paperwork over to you since I'm responsible for all of the money. Would you mind if I brought the papers over to your house?"

"No," Michael replied. "I wouldn't mind at all."

"How about tonight?" Brenda pressed. "I could bring them tonight."

Michael hesitated. "I guess tonight is as good as any."

"Good," Brenda said. "I'll see you about seven thirty."

"Alright." Michael grabbed one of Laura's hands and kissed it. "It was good seeing you, Miss Laura. But I better hurry. I've got an appointment in about thirty minutes. I was hoping to run in here, pick up a couple of things, and get right on out."

"Alright, Michael," Laura replied. "It's good seeing you, too."

"Take care." Michael turned and began to walk away.

"See you tonight," Brenda confirmed.

He glanced back and said, "Tonight," before he disappeared around the corner of the aisle.

Brenda and Laura completed their grocery shopping. But Laura was unusually quiet. Brenda chattered to fill the void. They hadn't been back home five minutes before Laura put the reason for her silence on the table.

"What in the world did you call yourself doing in the grocery store?"

"What?" Brenda replied.

"Don't what me, Brenda Robinson. All that smiling and smooth talking you were doing with Michael."

"I wasn't doing any smooth talki—"

"Yes, you were. If that wasn't smooth talking I've never heard any. And the way you looked when you saw him . . . If Michael had had a piece of bread in his hand, he could have spread you just like peanut butter."

Brenda placed the dried macaroni in the cabinet. "Now Mama, you're sounding ridiculous."

"No more ridiculous than you looked." Laura pressed her lips together. "I want you to know that."

Brenda just looked at her.

"Have you been seeing Michael?"

"I've seen him at some of the neighborhood meetings, and at a few other social gatherings. But I know what you mean." Brenda placed her hand on her hip. "And why would you ask me that?"

"Why?" Laura retorted. "You know why. Michael is Cora's man, and you don't mess around with your sister's man."

"My goodness." Brenda put her other hand on her hip. "This speech is a little late, isn't it? Why didn't you tell Cora that?"

"There was no need."

"Well Michael was definitely Annette's before Cora got a hold of him."

"But Annette's gone." Laura's eyes narrowed. "And where she's gone to ain't nothing going to become of her relationship with Michael. But you and Michael, that's another thing. It's Michael and Cora now. And you need to remember that."

"Michael and Cora? Mama, Cora has been gone a year and a half. And the last time I spoke to Michael about it, which was a couple of weeks ago, he hadn't heard one word from her. Not one word from Cora since she's been gone. Not one phone call. Not one letter. Nothing. And on that subject, how much have we heard from her? How many letters have you gotten, Mama. Five? Three? Two?"

"We don't know what Cora's doing or if she can even get a letter out from there. You should be more concerned about your sister's welfare than judging her based on how many letters she's written."

Brenda closed the cabinet door. "She wouldn't have to write if she hadn't left. Now we know that for sure. We wouldn't have to worry about her either."

A pained look crossed Laura's face, but it quickly disappeared. "You know, there's no need for me to talk to you about Cora. No need at all. Because the truth is you are jealous of her and you always have been." She crossed her arms. "And I think that's why you're going after Michael."

Brenda reared back. "Jealous! I am not jealous! Why should I be? For as long as I can remember, Cora has always been doing things I would never think of doing."

"And that's why. Cora is free enough to be herself and—"

"And I'm just what, Mama? So uptight I can't be myself?" Brenda drew her body up to its fullest height. "I am who I am, and I happen to feel good about myself. But I wish that you felt good about me. But no matter how I've tried, I've never been able to make you love me the way you love Cora. Well you know what?" She shook her head. "I'm sick of trying. And from this day forward I'm never going to try again. If you prefer to defend and to give all of your heart to Cora, who has proven to be irresponsible, self-ish"—her voice broke—"a liar and even a whor—"

"You stop right there." Laura's arm shot straight out. "You stop right there. Don't you dare speak like that in my house. Don't you dare!"

"You don't have to worry." Tears ran down Brenda's cheeks. "I won't speak like that in *your* house. But why not? You won't go to church. You won't get involved with *my* committee just because it's associated with the church. How do you think that makes me feel, Mama? How can I encourage other people to get involved with Community Ties when I can't even convince my own mother?"

Laura's chin jutted out. "I've never been to one of your meetings and I don't intend to. And I'm going to tell you something, don't you ever use that tone with me again in my house." She drew an agitated breath. "Or speak like that again about anyone, and definitely not your sister. If you got to talk like that, you can just stay out of here. You hear me?"

Brenda's face quivered as she stood with stiff arms at her side. "I hear you and understand you very well, Mama. And I'm going to get some clothes and do just that."

Laura stood in the kitchen and listened as Brenda gathered her things in the bedroom upstairs. When the front door closed, her body trembled inside, but she did not go to the door and call her child back. Instead, Laura slowly made her way upstairs. "I'm just not going to have it. It's not right. Brenda's always had a problem with Cora. What am I suppose to do? Cora is a good child. She's been a good girl. She's just not like Brenda, and Brenda has never understood that."

Laura reached the last step and her head started to swim. She tried to pull herself up, but her vision blurred and she grabbed empty air instead. Laura gasped and tumbled down the stairs.

Nebia's Story . . .

"Was she hurt real bad?" Erica asked.

"Bad enough," Nebia replied. "You see, I was the one who found her. I heard all this noise and I had a feeling something dreadful had happened. I went and knocked on Laura's door, and when she didn't come I called out to her. I heard her call my name. She sounded weak, so I went inside. And there she was, just one big, crying heap on the floor. Did she cry that day . . ." Nebia shook her head. "I think she cried about everything when it came to her children and her life, too. Her youngest was dead, her middle child was gone in a way that she didn't know how to call her back, and how she had never really been able to hold her eldest close to her heart."

"Why was that, Miss Nebia?" Cynthia held her face in her hands.

"To be honest, I think it was because Brenda looked so much like Steve. Like her father."

"That wasn't Brenda's fault," Cynthia replied.

"No, it wasn't. And of course Laura knew that, and that's why it ate at her so. Because she really did love Brenda."

The porch grew quiet, then Nebia continued.

"Laura cried for her own life, too. All the sacrifices she had made to raise her girls right, to try to make life for them better than what she'd had. I think while she lay there helpless on the floor, she realized her whole life had slipped to the wayside. Laura hadn't given herself the kind of attention she needed, and that's what the doctors told her. They told Laura her sugar was bad. Real bad. And—duh . . . you know, after her bruised leg didn't heal the doctors told her it was because of the sugar." Nebia focused ahead. "That leg never acted right after that, and Laura had to use a walker around the house. Sometimes when we went out she had to be in a wheelchair."

"Oh no," Sheila said.

"Ye-es, life can deal some hard blows sometimes," Nebia replied.

"But a lot of times it's just to get our attention. If we paid attention before the tragedy, I think most outcomes would be less painful."

"But what about Brenda? Did she come back and stay with her mother?" Erica inquired.

"No." Nebia chewed on her lip. "No. Laura didn't even want Brenda to know how badly she had hurt herself. She just shut her out. Hm-hm-hm. That argument hurt both of them. It hurt both of them real bad."

Chapter 14

"I don't want to get up," Brenda said with her eyes closed. "What time is it?"

"It's two twelve," Michael replied. "I guess we fell asleep."

"Obviously." Brenda sighed and removed her arm which rested across Michael's chest.

They lay in silence.

"I think I'll count to three. That'll help me get up." Brenda yawned. One . . . two . . . th—"

"Don't go," Michael said softly. "I don't want you to have to drive home this time of morning. Just stay here. We'll get up early enough for you to go home and change clothes for work."

"You won't get any resistance out of me." Brenda relaxed and propped herself up on her elbow. She faced Michael, who had his eyes closed. "So I'm actually going to get to spend the night here."

"Sure." Michael glanced at her before he closed his eyes again. "You could have spent the night before."

She picked at his pillow slip. "I knew I could have, but I wanted to be invited."

"I guess I'm a little slow sometimes."

Brenda looked at the ceiling. "At least let me salvage some respect."

Michael's eyes opened. "I respect you. You know that. Respect is not even an issue."

She touched his face. "I know that. But I wonder how many other people do."

"What?"

"You kno-ow. People tend to talk. And we have quite a history."

"Yeah, I guess people are talking." Michael looked at her. "From the outside this probably looks pretty messy."

"Well . . ." Brenda paused. "We can fix that."

"And how do you propose we do that?"

"By you making a respectable woman out of me. By you marrying me, Michael."

Michael looked away.

"Is just the thought of it so bad that you have to turn your face away?" Pain was in her voice.

Michael pulled Brenda close. "No. It's not that. I just don't know if it would work."

"Of course it would work," Brenda encouraged. "We are two good people with good hearts. You're a hard-working man and I'm a hard-working woman. We care about our community and we care about each other." She shook her hair that resembled locks in the dark. "So many people get married with much less than that."

Michael watched Brenda as she talked. Even after Brenda was done Michael continued to stare.

"Why are you looking at me like that?"

"You . . . you look like . . ."

"I look what?"

"No. I—I just—" He couldn't bring himself to tell her the truth. That for a moment with the shadow and the moonlight she looked so much like Cora. "Get married." Michael closed his eyes again. "You look so sure. What would your mother think about this?"

"It's not Mama's decision." Brenda's tone was edgy. "She's got her life and we've got ours. The day I left, I told myself I would not live my life for my mother or my sisters anymore. That I had to do what makes me happy. Regardless of what they think."

Michael looked at a small woven container Cora had given him. "So in other words, Miss Laura wouldn't be too happy."

"The truth is I don't know. Once in a while I go by there. But she treats me so cold, Michael, I just can't stand it. I'm tired of beating my head up against that wall. Whatever battle Mama's got going on inside of her I can't do anything about it. But I can live my life. And I want to marry you, Michael. I want a family. I want children. Don't you?"

"Yes I do."

Michael's bedroom went silent again.

"Did you want a wedding?" Michael asked softly.

Brenda's eyes brightened, even in the dark. "Just a simple ceremony. We can get dressed up and go down to the courthouse. Maybe we can have someone close to us be a witness."

"Maybe your mother would agree to that."

Brenda looked down. She shook her head. "I wouldn't count on it."

"I see," Michael replied. "Her or Miss Nebia would come, wouldn't they?"

"You never know with Nebia." Brenda replied. "I think the only reason she might not come is because of Mama. But we can always ask Miss Lucille."

"No. We'll just get dressed and go down there ourselves. I'm sure there's somebody there who can act as a witness." It was almost a whisper.

"Yes. Yes, we can. As a matter of fact, we can go down there this afternoon and get it over with. It's almost the end of the month. I can give notice at my place and move on in here."

Michael paused a split second. "Sounds like a plan," he replied.

"Oh Michael!" Brenda wrapped her arms around him. "I'm going to make you the happiest husband in all of St. Petersburg."

"I want you to be happy too, Brenda." He put his arms around her and held her tight. "I'll do everything I can to make you happy."

But his eyes went again to the woven African container on the edge of his nightstand.

Nebia's Story . . .

"They got married!" Cynthia couldn't believe it.

"Yes, they did," Nebia replied. "When I heard about it the deed had been done."

Sheila shook her head. "Did they invite Miss Laura?"

"From what she told me, Brenda invited her. But Laura said she told her she wasn't doing anything but digging a hole of sorrow in marrying Michael."

"No she didn't." Sheila sat back in her chair.

"Michael was absolutely tripping," Cynthia said. "It seems like he had this thing where he really wanted Cora so bad that Brenda was the nearest substitute. And that's horrible."

"You could look at it that way," Nebia replied. "But some folks believe in karma."

"Karma?" Sheila questioned.

"You're talking about what you sow you going to reap. Whatever cause you make you're going to get the result, good or bad." Cynthia replied.

"That's about right. But I don't believe it's so simple," Nebia explained. "I believe we're born over and over again, making causes all the while. That we come back here surrounded by the same souls. I believe Michael had lifetimes with the Robinsons, and he was working out something this time that was so old that neither his mind nor his heart understood why he did some of the things he did."

"You can blame it on karma or whatever," Erica said. "But I say that man had no self-restraint. No morals whatsoever."

Nebia shrugged. "But this is the same man, when Laura's bathroom flooded and the floorboards were so weak she couldn't bring the wheelchair or the walker in there to bathe herself, who secretly backed the loan she had been turned down for. Michael never told Laura that."

"So he really did have a good heart." Sheila sat forward again.

"Ye-es, he did. And it was open." Nebia scratched her arm. "Maybe too open for his own good."

Chapter 15

"Hello-o. Anybody home?" Lucille rapped on Laura's door again. "Laura, you in there?"

Finally, Nebia came to the door.

"How you doing, Miss Nebia?" Lucille inquired as she entered.

"Just fine," Nebia said as she turned her back and walked toward the kitchen. "Laura's back here."

"I'm dropping in for a minute," Lucille explained as she followed Nebia. "I'm not going to take up too much of her time. I know she hasn't been feeling all that well, and must be worn out after the big day today. Hello," Lucille said cheerily when she saw Laura. "How you doing?"

"I'm doin' fair to middlin', as they say," Laura replied. "I've been better." She leaned heavily on her walker as she made her way to a chrome framed kitchen chair. "But it's also been worse." Laura dropped into the chair.

"I thought you might still be dressed," Lucille said.

"Dressed?" Laura looked confused.

"Yes. I got off the bus at Tenth South and who was coming up on the side street? Brenda and Michael with 'Just Married' painted on the back window." Her smile broadened. "I waved them down and they pulled over. I was so surprised to see them! I told them I was mad because they didn't invite me to the wedding, but Brenda explained it was a really simple ceremony. That you all went down to the courthouse and did it." Lucille waved her hand. "So I didn't feel too bad. And Brenda said there was no reception or anything. That you just had a little something to eat afterwards. So . . ." She shrugged.

The kitchen was heavy with silence, but Lucille didn't notice.

"So what time were you at the courthouse?" she asked.

"I haven't been to no courthouse today," Laura replied.

"What?" Lucille looked at Laura, then at Nebia. "But I could have sworn that Brenda said that they got married at the courthouse."

"She might have." Laura's shoulder jerked. "I said I haven't been to no courthouse today. I don't know what Brenda and Michael's done."

"Come on. Laura, you mean to tell me that you didn't go to your own daughter's wedding?"

"I didn't receive an invitation," Laura replied.

"I can't believe this." Lucille sat down at the table.

"Now, tell the truth now," Nebia said. "You didn't receive an invitation because you didn't want one."

Laura leaned back.

"Either way, I didn't get one," Laura replied.

"It wouldn't have hurt you none to have at least spoken to her about it." Nebia took the dishes from the counter and placed them in the sink. "Brenda came over here, then she came upstairs asking me where you were. I hate to lie." She turned on the faucet. "I told her I thought you were in here asleep. But I knew you were in here being stubborn and not answering the door. You know you don't do things like that, Laura, and it don't come back on you."

"I didn't want nothing to do with their wedding. Nothing at all. She went against my word when she decided to marry Michael, and Brenda knew that I wasn't coming."

Nebia added liquid detergent to the water. "Yeah, and an old, stiff tree don't do well in a storm," Nebia warned. "You get a lot of wind blowing and it's going to break. It's best to learn to bend a little bit sometimes."

"Well I didn't see you going, since you thought it was such a good idea. I didn't see you taking yourself up there," Laura retorted.

"And have you not speaking to me, too? You need somebody to help you around here."

"I don't need no help. I do just fine." Laura folded up her walker as if to hide the evidence of her lie. "Children. You give them everything you have. Then they go their separate ways and forget everything you ever taught them. And then think you are the enemy," Laura mumbled. "How can the womb that gave them life be the enemy?"

"Sometimes it's the womb that needs to realize it shouldn't expect so much from those that come from it. It's just a place of birth. All they suppose to give back is love, and—"

"How you know so much about children?" Laura glared at Nebia. "You have never had a child in your life. So don't stand up there and start telling me about children. I—"

"Speaking of children." Lucille jumped in between them. "I had a wonderful surprise yesterday. Warren sent me another package and another letter. He's been so good over the years trying to help take care of his mama. See there, all children aren't bad, Laura." She lightened the atmosphere. "I tell you, my boy has seen parts of this world that I never dreamed of seeing. Some of them I didn't even know existed. Right now he's in the Philippines, but because of some kind of chest problem he's going to be coming home soon. His medical condition kept him from being sent to Vietnam, thank God." She smacked her hands together. "And he'll be coming back here to St. Petersburg to settle down because he knows I don't have nobody else."

"Warren was always a good boy anyway." Laura looked down. "I'm glad for you, Lucille. That he's bringing you some happiness. We all deserve it, don't we?"

"Sure we do." Lucille touched Laura's hand. "You want to see his picture?"

"You got a picture of him?"

"Right here." Lucille unsnapped her pocketbook and dug inside. She removed the photograph, with loving care, from a folded handkerchief. "Here he is all dressed up in his uniform. If he wasn't my child I'd say he's one of the handsomest young men I've ever seen." Slowly, as if she couldn't bear to let go of the snapshot, Lucille passed it to Laura.

"My goodness. He is a good-looking young man, Lucille. Very good-looking. I tell you he's a sight for sore eyes."

Nebia leaned over Laura's shoulder. "A mighty sight. Mighty."

Laura returned the photo to Lucille and then made a show of picking at her nails. "Did Brenda say where they were going?"

Nebia and Lucille's eyes met.

"No, she didn't. But I didn't ask." Lucille focused on Laura's downcast head. "But oh-h, did she look pretty. She had this hat with little blue flowers all over it. It was classy, too. You know Brenda has always been such a class act. And the dress she had on matched it perfectly." Lucille paused for a moment. "She looked happy, Laura."

"I hope it lasts." Laura continued to look down. Then she looked up slowly. "I really do. But something just don't feel right around none of it. That's all I know."

"We need to let the future work itself out," Nebia replied. "All we can do, is do the best right here and now."

Two big fat tears rolled down Laura's face.

"Oh, Laura," Lucille consoled her. "There's no need for that." She took a napkin from the old napkin holder and gave it to Laura.

Laura dabbed at her eyes.

"We all do things that we regret. When Brenda comes back, you can tell her that you wish you had gone to the wedding, and that you wish her well."

"But see, that's the problem." Laura crushed the napkin in her hand. "I don't wish I was at the wedding. I want Brenda to be happy.

And I want Michael to be happy. But the two of them together . . ."
She shook her head. "There's something in my heart that just
won't—can't accept it. I don't know if it ever will."

Nebia's Story . . .

"That is so sad." Erica gazed at the night sky. "It's so sad. Here
she is, couldn't even acknowledge her own daughter was getting
married. And even though Laura was hurting, there was something
blocking her heart so tough, she couldn't even wish them well.
That's sad."

"And Laura was sad too," Nebia replied. "But there didn't seem
to be nothing she could do about it. Nothing at all. You're right.
Something deep inside of her was the root of it all. And even when
I tried to help her she couldn't hear me."

"So were Michael and Brenda happy?" Sheila asked.

"From what I heard they were. But I only saw them once in
awhile. Still, in a neighborhood you'd hear things. For instance, I
heard they were doing well, and people in the community seemed
to look up to them. Michael's business was growing like wildfire,
and I got to believe a lot of that had to do with Brenda. Brenda
worked hard to make her marriage work, and to help Michael be
successful. So, I would say she was happy to a certain extent. But
you know, some wise folks say happy is just a time between two
points of sadness, and sadness is just a time between two points of
happiness. Life goes on. It's not always pretty, but it goes on."

Chapter 16

"**B**renda. I'm home," Michael called.

"Hi, Baby," Brenda replied from the dining room. She had worked a half day. There was an appointment that afternoon that she did not want to miss.

Anxious, Brenda glanced at the dining room door. She had asked Michael to call right before he left the office so everything could be timed perfectly. With precision, Brenda struck the match-book and lit the two candles. "How was your day?" She continued to engage Michael as his approaching footsteps sounded on the hardwood floors.

"Great!" he replied. "Where are you? I got something to tell you."

"I'll be right there." Brenda looked at the curtains that had been drawn to set a romantic mood. Then at the table that was set with their best china, silverware, and napkins, before she flipped off the light and hurried to intercept Michael.

"Hi, Baby," she repeated. "You sound excited." She put her arms around his neck and gave him a kiss. Brenda closed her eyes as Michael squeezed her. "Seems like this is a special day all around."

"You can say that again." Michael smiled. "We picked up a record number of customers today, but outside of that . . ." He grabbed her forearms. "I've got a surprise for you."

"You do?" Brenda giggled. "I guess this is also a day for surprises." She took his briefcase from his hand and placed it on the floor before she led Michael toward the dining room.

"Okay, here it goes." Michael shook his finger as they walked. "I've been waiting and waiting and waiting to see if this guy was going to accept an impromptu but serious offer that I made."

"What offer?" Brenda asked as they stood outside the back entrance to the dimly lit dining room.

"We're going to buy another piece of property," Michael exploded. "Our second piece of property, Brenda. You know how we've been discussing it, well, a great deal has finally come our way. The building will need renovating, of course, and your approval," Michael said with his face full of anticipation.

"That's wonderful, Michael." Brenda hugged him again.

"It is." Michael burst into another smile. "And it's only the beginning, because we're going to buy more and more, and we, as the Dawsons, might single-handledly renovate this part of St. Pete."

Brenda's smile dimmed a bit. "Wow. It sounds good, but extremely ambitious." She glanced at the romantic table inside the room. "But honey?"

"What?"

"What do you think?"

Brenda lifted her arm toward the dining table.

"Now, this is wow!" Michael said as he looked at the room and the table for the first time. "This is beautiful, Brenda." He kissed her forehead. "Looks like I'm in for quite a treat tonight."

"We're in for a treat." Brenda assured him. "And I fixed your favorite food. Meatloaf with gravy and mashed potatoes. Green beans." She lifted her chin with pride. "And I even made a peach cobbler."

"No, you didn't!" Michael smiled mischievously.

"Yes, I did. Can't you smell it?" She waved her hand in front of his nose.

"I can. And now I'm instantly hungry."

"Good." Brenda's enthusiasm continued to rise. "Well, you take off your coat and get relaxed, and I'll bring all the food out. We'll just dine from the middle of the table and celebrate."

"You are wonderful." Michael pecked Brenda on the lips. "It's like you knew that this was going to be a special day in our lives."

"It is a special day, Michael." Her eyes glistened. "It really is."

Moments later they were seated at the table, serving themselves while Michael continued to chatter about the acquisition he planned to make.

"And this is quite the building. It needs some work, but it's beautiful, Brenda. And if we turn it over right away, I think we could make a nice little chunk of change off of this one. But who knows, maybe we'll just keep it and rent it out, because it has four units. It's a fourplex. And the truth is I can see it as a possible long-term source of income for us."

Brenda chewed and listened, listened and chewed as Michael went on.

"So of course with this kind of purchase we must watch our money now. We're going to need extra cash to put into the building to bring it up to par. So whatever you do, honey, watch the shopping, don't bring in any new things, at least not for a minute."

Brenda looked down. "What's a minute, Michael?"

"I'd say, let's give ourselves about six to nine months of not making any big purchases, because we don't want to increase our debt. We're doing great, but just to be on the safe side I'd rather have more money than what we'll need for the renovations, than to have just enough, because you never know what you may come across when you get involved with this kind of project."

"I can imagine." Brenda's face looked drained.

"But don't worry. You've done a great job of managing our money, and I know that at this important time you will do just the same."

Brenda placed her forehead in her hand. "Michael, as you said, you know that I've always supported you in whatever you've done to make our lives as rich as they are." She looked around the well-furnished room. "I'm all about that."

"I know," Michael replied.

"So-um. I just don't know what to say right now." Brenda shook her head. "There's already something that's in the works that probably will call for more money than we've ever needed."

Michael stopped eating. "Like what?"

"Well, like . . ." Brenda hesitated. "I didn't want to tell you this way."

"You didn't want to tell me what this way?" Michael sat back. "What are you talking about?"

"I didn't want to tell you during a business discussion that we're having a baby. We're having a baby, Michael."

"A baby." Michael repeated the words.

"Ye-es. A baby." Brenda's eyes softened.

"A baby." Michael looked down. "My goodness. I just don't know what to say." He looked up. "It's wonderful. I mean . . . it truly is, but at the same time we promised that we would not start having children for a couple of years."

"I know that." Brenda looked hurt. "But . . . Michael you work so much and everything. I just . . . and I'm working, too. I mean our lives are so busy with business, I just felt as if a baby would make us closer, would make our home more of a home. You'd be around the house a little more, around me a little more and . . ."

"Brenda, I'm around you a lot, we work together."

"But it's not the same thing. Working together and being at home as a family is not the same thing," she pleaded.

"I know that." Michael took another forkful of meatloaf and then a deep breath.

"Michael, even though I know we agreed, I thought that you would be happy that we were having a child. I really did. I guess I was wrong."

"You're not wrong." He touched her hand across the table. "I just . . . I just wasn't expecting this at this time . . . when this project has come available. I'm thinking about the verbal commitment that I made."

"Well, but it's verbal. You haven't actually signed the papers for the building. And it's not that we don't have plenty of money, Michael. We can always buy another piece of property after the baby is born. You're such a go-getter, Michael, you'll be able to find another deal."

"But that's not promised. Something like this comes only once in a lifetime. I can't just walk away from it, and like I said, I've given my word."

Brenda's shoulder's drooped. "And an opportunity like this, a baby, this particular child born from us, comes only once in a lifetime, Michael. We can't walk away from it either. We are going to have this baby like it or not."

Brenda got up and walked away from the table as Michael called, "Brenda. Brenda."

Nebia's Story . . .

"Oh-h boy," Sheila remarked. "There's already signs of trouble in paradise."

"There were signs in the very beginning that there would be trouble," Nebia said. "But Brenda loved Michael so much she felt she had enough willpower to make things work. And she had enough love to make them work perfectly."

"But it didn't sound like Michael didn't want the baby." Erica said, "It sounded like, in his mind, it was bad timing because they had agreed not to have any children for a while."

"Obviously, they had agreed," Nebia replied. "But Brenda knew there was something missing in their marriage, and this was one of the ways she was trying to fill that gap."

"Did it work?" Cynthia asked.

"If only life was that simple," Nebia replied. "Then earth itself would be paradise, wouldn't it?"

Chapter 17

"Sh-sh-sh. Be quiet. Here come Mr. and Mrs. Dawson," a voice warned. Pastor Benson looked up from the papers in front of him.

"Well, good evening," the minister greeted them. "Glad to have you two back. You know you've spoiled us, Brenda. We can barely do anything without you." He patted her hand. "So it's good to see both of you. You're looking well."

"Thank you, Pastor Benson." Brenda looked nervous.

A chorus of "You look great, Mrs. Dawson," and "You've never looked better," circled through the church basement.

"Thank you," she said again, looking more embarrassed than ever.

Michael pulled one of the folding chairs out from beneath the table. Brenda sat down. Michael followed.

"We've got a small agenda today," Pastor Benson said. "And mainly it focuses around Community Ties. Are you prepared to give us an update on the situation, Brenda?"

She nodded. "Yes. The tutorial program is set up and ready for students. So you can put that in the church bulletin and we can get the word out. As far as the neighborhood watch goes, it's well on its way. We'll have another meeting next Friday." Brenda cleared her throat. "I know I haven't been very active over the last week or so. But I'm feeling up to the task again. And some of you can look forward to me contacting you." She looked around the table with a forced smile. "Because I'll need all the help that I can get." Brenda glanced at Michael then looked down.

The meeting continued, covering a few other issues, including a church bake sale scheduled for the upcoming weekend.

"Pauline, would you be in charge of the sale for us, please?" Pastor Benson asked. "Since you make the best German chocolate cake in St. Pete." He smiled.

"I'll be glad to," Pauline replied. "You know I'll do anything I can for the church. But I've got to bring up something that I know we are all dealing with right now."

"What's that?" Pastor Benson folded his hands on top of the table.

"This gang problem." Pauline looked at each face. "It's really beginning to affect our community. My boy, James, he come home the other night and I could tell he'd been crying, but he didn't want to talk to me about it. And when I finally forced him to tell me what was wrong, he told me he had been threatened by these gang members because he refused to join. They told him if he didn't join, they'd do something to my house, like set it on fire. This had him so upset. I can't tell you how long it had been since James had cried."

"I would think it would," Pastor Benson replied.

"But what scares me is it upset him so much he considered joining. We can't have our children being threatened like this."

"You're absolutely right." Pastor Benson looked down.

"And I tell you they're bringing dope in here, and they're selling it. Ain't no telling what all isn't going on," Pauline continued. "And the kids see that money, and you know, it's attractive to them when they compare it with folks who work like me, struggling hard just to make a living. It looks like easy money. It's all I can do to hold on to my child and let him know there is a better life, but he's got to go about it through education. The proper way."

"This is where Community Ties can come in." Brenda spoke up. "To help your son realize there are opportunities for him outside of this neighborhood if he prepares himself. Take the tutoring program, for instance. If James is not feeling strong in English, or in his communication skills, the tutoring program can make him stronger. And of course the neighborhood crime watch will help us band together against this negative element that is coming into our community. We do want our streets to be safe for our children." Brenda's voice faltered.

"And don't worry, Ms. Harris. I know some of those boys in the gangs, and their parents. I'll talk to the parents about it," Michael said. "I'll see if they'll willing to help in any kind of way."

"Would you, Mr. Dawson? You're such a great man. An inspiration. We all look up to you."

Michael put up his hand. "No, I just—"

"We do," Pauline insisted. "You've done some of the best things I've seen done in this community in a long, long time. You've been like a beacon here. You started that insurance company and made a way for lots of us to get insurance at rates that we wouldn't have been able to get. Then you opened your loan company. And I tell you, I know I wouldn't have my house today if it wasn't for you, and I thank you with all my heart."

Michael looked in her eyes. "You're welcome."

"So I know if you talk to them boys, maybe to some of their fathers that I know don't come to church and some of them may not have the best intentions themselves. But maybe still they'll listen to you."

"I'll try," Michael replied.

"That's right," Pastor Benson chimed. "We can definitely try to bring this community together, by being instruments of the Lord.

We can try to uplift it while the Lord watches over us and guides us."

"Amen" rose from the end of the table.

The meeting broke up. Cake and punch was served. Brenda took one of the smallest pieces and stepped over into a quiet spot. She nibbled slowly on the cake. A few minutes later Pauline joined her.

"I just want you to know I was sorry to hear what happened."

"I appreciate that." Brenda couldn't look in her face. "But I'm okay."

"I truly understand," Pauline continued. "I want you to know that. You see it's happened to me before, but I have four children now. So don't be discouraged because this was your first baby. Sometimes your body just got to get accustomed to carrying a child."

Brenda looked into Pauline's encouraging eyes. "I guess so."

She patted Brenda's hand. "So you take heart."

"I will," Brenda said with water in her eyes.

She watched Pauline walk away. Brenda hoped no one else would come over with condolences because she didn't know if she would be able to take it. Before they could, Brenda wrapped the remainder of her cake in her napkin and walked over to Michael. He was in the middle of a conversation. "I'm ready to go if you are," she interrupted.

Michael looked at her strained face. "Sure. We can go right now if you want."

Brenda nodded.

They said their good-byes and climbed up the stairs and went out into the parking lot. Michael opened the car door for Brenda before he climbed into the driver's seat.

"Pauline came over to me to give her condolences." Brenda sighed, heavily. "I don't think I could have stood it if anyone else had come up and told me they were sorry about my losing the baby." She paused. "And Lord knows I didn't want to just break down and start crying in the front of everybody. I thought I was stronger than

I am right now. I stayed away for a week, but I guess I still am hurting from it."

Michael touched her cheek. "And more than likely you're going to be. But don't worry. It'll pass."

"Michael." Brenda focused imploring eyes on his face. "I want us to work on having another baby as soon as possible. I think that would really help me."

Michael looked at the steering wheel. "I think it's a little early for that."

"It's my body," Brenda replied too quickly. "And I think I should be the judge of that."

"But Dr. Mills said you need to let your body build back up, and that we need to hold off doing everything because of the complications that you went through. Remember?"

For a moment Brenda was quiet, then her lip trembled. "If you don't want to make love to me, Michael, you don't have to use what the doctor said as an excuse."

Michael rubbed his forehead. "That's not why I said that. Please." He shook his head. "Don't start."

"Don't start what?" Tears spilled down her cheeks. "Don't you think I can tell? We've been married for one year and you barely think of touching me. I have to come to you. You don't desire me, Michael. I can feel it."

"That's not true. I . . ." He looked straight ahead.

"Look. I don't want to argue about it." Brenda sniffed. "I really don't. All I know is, I feel that when I have our baby we'll be closer. That whatever is holding you back from loving me completely, Michael, will be small in comparison to our having a child."

Michael took a deep breath. "All right." He turned to her. "I don't know what's wrong with me. But if you feel that a baby will make that big of a difference for us, I want one too. But," he added shaking his index finger, "I want you to get stronger first. I want you to be strong so that you can carry the baby to term, and things can be

just like you want them to be. Okay?" Michael searched her eyes.
"Let's give it a little time."

Brenda looked down at her hands that were clenched tightly in
her lap.

Finally she said, "Alright. But I don't want to wait too long."

Nebia's Story . . .

"Brenda had a miscarriage." Cynthia sat back with her arms held
tightly against her abdomen.

"Yes. Yes, she did," Nebia replied.

"How far along was she?"

"Almost three months. While it was happening she actually sent
for me. She thought I could do something about it." Nebia exhaled.
"Perhaps stop it with my herbs. But in her heart, she already knew
it was too late. Her pride wouldn't let her call the doctor, although
Michael made her go see him afterwards."

"Poor thing," Erica said.

"Ye-es, she was pretty pitiful around then."

"Did Laura come and see her?" Sheila asked.

"No-o, that woman was as stubborn as a mule. She didn't come
see her, but she picked me about her every opportunity that she
got. I told Laura she needed to go herself but she wouldn't go."
Nebia lit another brown cigarette. "But in Laura's defense I got to
say it was difficult for her to get around. Real difficult. By then they
had amputated her leg, just below the knee."

"Oh, no," Cynthia exclaimed.

"They had to. That sugar wouldn't let that wound heal. They
had to cut it off, and they did." Nebia blew a stream of smoke into
the air. "And Laura was down about that, real down. They sent her
for therapy, and—uh . . . she was given one of them legs. Pr-pra—"

"A prosthesis?" Sheila said.

"Yes, yes, that's what they called it. But Laura didn't like to use it.

When she was around the house she refused to. She said it was too heavy. Laura said it was more of a burden than a help."

"So basically she was confined to the wheelchair," Erica replied.

"Basically, she was," Nebia agreed.

"My goodness, Miss Nebia"—Sheila shook her head—"life wasn't going too good for the Robinsons, was it?"

"For a while there it seemed like there was a pretty dark cloud that had descended on them. And it looked like nobody could see through it. But just like the sun that can burn too hot but is needed, Cora came back again."

Chapter 18

"Aw-w, shoot!" Laura said. She whirled her wheelchair toward the stove and turned off the flame beneath the overflowing pot. "Nebia! Nebia!" Laura grabbed the sawed-off broom and hit it against the ceiling as the stew continued to spill over onto the range top and down the front of the stove.

As Laura focused on controlling the hot stream of stew, she did not hear the side door that was usually left unlocked for Nebia to come and go, open. She rolled to the kitchen sink and grabbed a drying towel before she returned to the stove to soak up the hot liquid. Laura stretched and spread the towel on the top of the range. "They make these stoves too doggone tall. How folks like me suppose to be able to clean them off? But no, they not thinking about me."

Right then, a warm hand covered hers and took the towel.

"Let me do it, Mama."

Laura looked up into Cora's face. Cora leaned forward and kissed her mother on the cheek. "I've got it." She took control of the situation as Laura sat back in stunned silence. When Cora was done, she turned to her mother.

"You're back." Laura found her voice. "I never thought this day would come again. I hoped that it would, but I just wasn't sure, and Cora . . ." She beamed. "You're as bright as the day you left."

"Mama." Cora dropped to her knees, and placed her head in her mother's lap. "And this time I'm home for good."

"It's a great day." Laura patted Cora's locked hair. "A great day."

They stayed that way as they shared tears. Then Cora sat back on her haunches. She looked at her mother's aged face, and then at the wheelchair. "What happened?"

Laura shook her head. "I had a fall one day and with my sugar being so bad I guess my leg never healed right. So they had to take it, Cora."

Cora's tears started again.

But Laura sat up straighter. "There's no need for that. I've been doing fine. Just fine. And they gave me a prosthesis that I know how to use real good. Isn't that right, Nebia?" Laura looked at Nebia who had entered the kitchen.

Nebia affirmed the lie with a slow nod, but her eyes were locked on Cora.

"Nebia." Cora stood up. She went over and took Nebia's gnarled hands in hers.

"Has she? Or did I abandon everyone at a time when you needed me most?"

Nebia opened her mouth to answer but Laura cut her off.

"Abandon? There's no need for that word. You didn't abandon nobody, Cora. I've been doing just fine. Nebia. Get my leg for me so I can strap it on and show Cora there's no need to talk like that."

Nebia turned to do as Laura asked. Her face was expressionless. It did not betray her friend.

"My plan is to lose a little weight, Cora. My size makes it a little more difficult for me to get around. But I'm going to do it. And now that you're back that's just the encouragement that I need. But you go on and take your things upstairs. Nebia and I will finish up in here. Dinner's almost ready anyway."

Cora hesitated.

"Go on and put them up," Laura insisted.

It took two trips for Cora to place her suitcases in her old bedroom. When she returned downstairs Cora saw the prosthesis in the corner. She looked at her mother, who was setting the table from the wheelchair. Nebia was dishing out the stew. "None of Brenda's things were in the room. Did she move out?"

"Yes," Laura replied. "She moved awhile back."

"Where?" Cora was shocked. "Is she still in St. Pete?"

"Um-hmm." Laura concentrated on placing the plate on the table.

Cora's eyes narrowed. "Then why did she move? It seems you need her around here more than ever. I know you've been helping, Nebia, but—"

"Every way I can," Nebia replied.

"It just doesn't seem like Brenda," Cora persisted.

Laura put another plate of beef stew and biscuits down. "Brenda got married, Cora."

Cora gasped. "Brenda is married." Her mouth spread into a smile. "I should have known that she would be the first one between the two of us to do it. Don't tell me she's a mother, too?" Her brow wrinkled. "I've missed so much."

Laura shook her head. "No. No, she's not a mother."

"Well who did she marry? Do we know him?" Cora looked from her mother to Nebia. "Tell me!"

Laura sat back in her wheelchair. She looked into Cora's eyes. "She married Michael, Cora."

"Michael." Cora repeated softly. "Brenda married Michael." She looked down at the floor.

For a moment no one spoke, and then Cora said, "I guess life just kind of comes full circle, huh? Brenda was the first to meet Michael, to care about him, so maybe it's right that she was the one that married him." Cora looked into Laura's stern face. "If there is one thing I've learned, it is to embrace whatever life gives you. Not to get too high with the highs, and too low with the lows. That won't change anything." Cora fell silent again. "I hope they're happy," she said softly. "I have to make sure that Brenda knows that."

"I don't know if they're happy or not," Laura replied. "I don't see much of them."

Cora's brow wrinkled again. "I can't believe Brenda would stay away knowing all that you're dealing with."

"It hasn't been Brenda. It's been me," Laura confessed.

"You?" Cora stopped in front of her mother. "I know you're not holding a grudge against Brenda because of Michael. I know you wouldn't do that, Mama. Not on account of me." Laura avoided Cora's probing gaze. "I was the one who left. I was the one who couldn't even be at Annette's funeral. Brenda's been the strong one. The one that's stood by your side. Who's been here through everything."

"I know," Laura finally replied. "I know what Brenda's done. It wasn't so much about you. It's just that I don't want to see another child of mine hurt. I don't know if I can stand it." Laura closed her eyes. "I wanted to protect her, but she wouldn't listen to me. And I decided I would not stand by and watch the pain come."

"Why are you so sure she's going to be hurt, Mama?" Cora looked down before she looked at her mother again. "Maybe Michael's the best thing that ever happened to Brenda. Maybe this is the happiness she deserves for trying to do what's right."

"Maybe." Laura's jaw set. "But only time will tell."

Nebia's Story . . .

"So Laura wasn't just trying to keep Brenda from marrying Michael because of Cora. She was doing it because she didn't want Brenda to get hurt," Erica said.

"I think that was part of it," Nebia replied. "But I think it wasn't totally true. I don't know if Laura really knew how much Cora was a part of how she treated Brenda. At the time I think she told herself it was true just so she could live with the decisions she made."

"You know . . ." Cynthia put her hands around her face. "I truly can't say—" She stopped, then started again. "Sometimes I've felt that my mother has favored Sheila over me, but I've never felt that she loved Sheila more than me."

"I feel I could say the same thing when it comes to you," Sheila said.

Cynthia continued, "I think Mama did a good job at making us both feel loved. So why is it, Miss Nebia, that Laura seemed to love Cora so much more than Brenda?"

"I think the word you used is right. Seemed," Nebia replied. "I don't think deep in her heart she did. It's just that Cora was what Laura had wanted to be. Wild and free. What the young Laura wanted to be. Back then she had so many dreams. Plus she had the ability, but Laura married early and the babies . . ." Nebia sucked her bottom lip. "The babies came so fast. She threw away her dreams and took care of her children despite all the things Steven was doing. I think part of Laura's self-esteem suffered while he was chasing them women. But instead of Laura wilting under that, she grew harder, and her anger became the fuel that kept her going." Nebia looked down. "But she loved Brenda. She really did."

"How did Cora look after being in Zambia so long?" Cynthia asked.

"Mighty well," Nebia replied. "She had matured, and she moved with the grace of a tigress. Surefooted. That's what she was, and finally grounded within herself. I didn't feel the nervousness that I had felt for her almost all of her life. I believe Cora had taken that part of her and turned it into a kind of strength. Like Laura had used her anger. Cora's hair was just below her shoulders." Nebia nodded. "Yes, Cora was a powerfully beautiful thing. That evening, I'll never forget it." Nebia patted her hands. "She pulled out all this cloth from Africa and she wrapped Laura's and my heads up in these mighty head wraps." Nebia laughed. "We played like children. It was so good to have Cora back. And I could tell she was truly happy to be home."

Chapter 19

Cora smacked her palm against her thighs. "I think it's time for me to go and see Brenda, Mama."

A shadow of guilt crossed Laura's face. "If that's what you want to do."

"It is," Cora replied. "I've been here three days. I don't want to just bump into her on the street. I've got to let her know I'm back." She stood up. "So you going to be okay?"

"I'll be just fine." Laura's expression was like that of an obstinate child.

"Then I'll see you shortly." Cora left the house.

At first she walked down the street in silence, but Cora began to talk to herself as she neared Brenda and Michael's home. "I want Brenda to know there are no hard feelings toward her because she married Michael." Her hand went over her heart. "But the truth is I hope we'll be able to talk alone without Michael being there. I only have one sister now, and our relationship as sisters is most important to me."

She focused on the sidewalk. "I don't want to think about Michael. He's Brenda's husband now, and that's all he will ever be."

Cora turned onto the street where Michael had restored his first house, and where she'd heard he'd bought two others. One house after another had been painted, and it was obvious several had been renovated. "Look-a-here. Michael said he'd do it. And he has."

A blue Oldsmobile 98 cruised by, and three curious sets of eyes locked on Cora. Cora stopped talking and stared back until the car passed. Moments later she walked up to Michael and Brenda's house. Two stone lions stood guard at the base of the concrete stairs, and an ornate beveled glass door surrounded by cherrywood sat in the middle. Cora stopped and took it all in before she climbed the stairs. When she reached the top, she bent over and picked up a newspaper just as the interior door opened. Cora looked up, straight into Brenda's eyes.

"Cora." Brenda unlocked the door.

"Hello." Cora smiled, a small sincere smile. "I've been back for three days now and I had to come by and say hello to my sister."

Brenda's look of surprise faded. "I'm glad you did." She opened the door. "Come in."

Cora stepped inside and glanced around. Everything looked new. The furniture and paintings were coordinated like pictures in a magazine.

"I got here a few minutes ago," Brenda informed her. "If you had come a minute or two earlier you would have missed me."

"So it worked out perfectly, didn't it?" Cora replied. Understanding was in both sets of eyes.

"Yes it did." Brenda led Cora to the living room. "Come in. Have a seat." They sat down on a classy mix of green and gold furniture.

"So you say you've been back three days now?" Brenda seemed nervous.

"Yes." Cora nodded.

"How are you?"

"I'm good." Cora tried to cut through the stilted atmosphere. "I'm good. I finally feel like I've come home, and I don't feel like I ever have to go away again." She sighed. "I'm glad to be here."

Brenda looked at the newspaper she held in her hand. "So I guess . . . it's obvious that . . ." She searched for the right words. "Michael and I are together. We're married now."

"Yes." Cora looked at the ring on Brenda's hand. "Yes, that is obvious. And of course Mama told me."

"Of course." Brenda nodded. "How is she?"

"She's making it." Cora crossed her legs. "Nebia helps out a lot, so they make do. But now that I'm back I'll try to do my part."

Brenda exhaled. "Cora, I want you to know it wasn't my idea not to help Mama."

"I know that." Cora reached forward and touched her hand. "And I understand. At least I think I do. Mama has her ways and what can you do about it? We've all made decisions and now we've got to live with them."

Brenda glanced at one of her paintings. "Yes, we do."

"How are you, Brenda?" Cora asked. "Are you happy?"

Brenda focused on Cora's face. A wisp of a smile rose and faded. "I've got a good life, Cora. Anything I want I pretty much can have. Michael is good to me. So what is there to be unhappy about?"

Cora nodded in the silence that followed.

Brenda slid to the edge of the couch. "I'm going to be fixing dinner shortly. Would you like to stay?"

"Oh, no." Cora shook her head. "I don't think that would be a good idea. I simply wanted to see you." She bit her lip. "I'm happy for you, Brenda. This is a strange situation for both of us, but God don't make no mistakes. We'll get through it. I believe things are just as they should be." She closed her eyes. "And I want you to know that."

A shaky hand rose to Brenda's mouth, then she dabbed at her eyes. "I'm glad you see it that way."

Cora walked over and put her arms around Brenda. "I gotta go."

"All right," Brenda replied.

"We'll see each other," Cora said as they walked toward the door.

"Yes, we will," Brenda agreed, but they made no plans.

Brenda squeezed Cora's hand.

"I thought I heard voices," Michael said as he entered the front hall.

Cora and Brenda turned.

"Evenin', honey." Brenda walked over and gave Michael a kiss on the cheek, but he didn't look at her. His eyes were fixed on Cora. "Cora!"

"Hello, Michael." Cora's arms hugged her sides. "I just came by to say hello. And to let—"

"When did you get back?" he interrupted her.

"A few days ago." Her gaze darted from Michael to Brenda.

Michael's eyes never left Cora's face. She reached for the doorknob.

"I know you're about to have dinner. So I better go. I'm eating at the house with Mama and Nebia."

"Sure. Sure," Michael said. He looked at Brenda for the first time.

"It was good to see both of you." Cora opened the door. "Take care." She closed the door behind her without looking back.

Nebia's Story . . .

"Whatever little bit of bond Cora and Brenda tried to recapture, Michael's reaction sure didn't help that any. My goodness. Why in the world was he standing up there staring like that?" Sheila said.

"See . . . that's what I'm talking about," Erica replied. "How can you like a man like that? He didn't have any control."

"Michael had control," Nebia replied. "But his heart still yearned for Cora. And it was the one thing that kept Brenda and Cora from really renewing their relationship. If Brenda could have believed that Michael no longer cared for Cora I think things would have gone smoother between them." Nebia's mouth turned down. "But Brenda never believed that because it wasn't true."

"So they just stayed away from each other," Sheila said.

"Let's say they didn't try to get together," Nebia replied. "There was a silent agreement that staying apart was better."

"I've got to wonder," Cynthia said. "Was Cora really being honest when she said she wished Michael and Brenda well? I just don't know about that, you know? That would be a hard pill to swallow. Sister and all."

"Of course it would," Nebia replied. "But I think that Cora realized that she never loved Michael the way Brenda did. And she wasn't certain that she would have been the kind of wife that Michael needed to be the social climber that he was. Cora wasn't into that kind of thing. Cora's way was outside the system." Nebia rubbed her eyes. "She wanted to revolutionize things. And I gotta admit, working inside the system, as far as Brenda and Michael were concerned, they were a perfect match."

"So what did Cora end up doing?" Cynthia inquired.

"Oh-h, she painted, and she actually sold a few of them. Cora also sold some of the things she brought back from Africa." Nebia pinched her nose. "And from time to time she'd import a few more and sell them too. But mostly Cora read a lot."

"Read a lot?" Erica sat back. "Cora was the one who didn't like school, right?"

"Yes, that's true. But time changes things."

"What kind of books did she read?" Cynthia asked.

"All kinds of books about life, different countries, different ways of thinking. Unlike when she was a little girl and she would come to me with a million questions, now Cora sought the answers on her own." Nebia squeezed her knees, and then grimaced. "Ye-es. You could find Cora reading on the beach or in the park. Then she'd be out there contemplatin' nature. That's what I called sitting with her eyes closed and all." Nebia smiled. "But Cora said she was meditating. A few kids would come and sit beside her and imitate what she was doing." She shook her head. "Cora was quite the colorful character in the neighborhood."

"And she was satisfied with that after the way she'd lived her life?" Cynthia looked skeptical.

"At that time she seemed satisfied to me," Nebia replied. "I think it was a time of processing for Cora. Looking back over and understanding the life she'd led. Everything she had experienced. All she knew. She'd gathered her life, blossoms and thorns, right there in her lap." Nebia patted her thigh. "Cora was content and still inside herself for the first time. And it opened her up in a way we would have never expected."

Chapter 20

"All I need is a pinch of salt. You don't have no salt in this place, Laura?" Nebia searched through the kitchen cabinets.

"Did you find any?" Laura retorted. "And what are you doing over there anyway? Why you putting that stuff in that cloth? And who's it for?"

"That's none of your business. I asked you for salt," Nebia replied.

"If you didn't find any, there isn't any." Laura looked at Cora. "Don't you have some in your own place?"

"I would have if I didn't have to bring it down here for you. And now you've cooked up all the salt and didn't tell nobody. Ain't no salt in the building nowhere."

"Well you should have bought some more." Laura turned her head.

"How could I know to buy—"

Cora burst out laughing.

"What you laughing about?" Laura's brow lowered.

"I'm laughing at the two of you. Arguing over salt."

A sheepish look crossed Laura's face. "Well the truth is, all that old stuff Nebia's putting in that cloth, it stinks. Absolutely stinks."

"The odor is part of the reason the bag works," Nebia threw back at her.

"Well, whoever is going to be wearing that thing around their neck won't only get rid of sickness, they'll keep everybody within ten miles away from them."

"All right now." Nebia gave Laura the eye. "You just remember this conversation when you want me to fix one up for you."

Laura looked somewhat remorseful. She scratched her nose. "I got to admit, your herbs have helped me more than once. So maybe I shouldn't be too harsh on you."

Nebia's shoulders softened. "Yeah well, at the moment that's not helping me none. I can't finish this without salt."

Cora got up. "I'll go see if Miss Lucille's got any. I'll be right back."

Cora rounded the back of the building and came up on the other side. She arrived at Lucille's door and tapped gently. Moments later it opened.

"Hey, Cora." Lucille beamed. "Come on in."

"Hi, Miss Lucille. I hope I'm not intruding on anything, but Mama and Nebia are up front arguing over there being no salt in the house." She stepped over the threshold. "I thought perhaps you'd have some."

"I sure do." A bright smile continued to dominate Lucille's face. "And I've got a surprise for you." She beckoned for Cora to follow her through the apartment, but before they could enter the kitchen, a uniform-clad Warren met them in the short hallway.

"Cora Robinson. I'd know that voice anywhere. Matured or not."

"Warren! Is this really you?" Cora looked him up and down. "I can't believe it. Oh my goodness!" Cora gave him the biggest hug, then she stepped back. "You look magnificent." She laughed.

"And so do you." Warren's eyes twinkled.

Cora looked down at her worn pair of jeans and old T-shirt. "Oh please. I don't look like you." She squinted toward the top of his head. "And my God, you grew."

"A few inches," Warren replied.

"How tall are you now?" Cora continued to smile.

"I'm six three."

"Six three." Cora shook her head. "I can't get over you. Look at that manicured haircut. And it just frames your face. Well, Miss Lucille . . ." Cora tore her gaze away from Warren. "This surely is a surprise. A big one."

Lucille's hands fluttered. "Why don't you two sit down and talk while I get the salt."

"I can't," Cora said. "Nebia's waiting. I really can't stay. But I wish I could." Cora smiled again.

"All right," Lucille replied. "I'll put you a little bit in a piece of aluminum foil."

"That'll be just fine," Cora said.

"Cora Robinson." Warren repeated when his mother left the room. "You look as wild as the day we sat on the back porch and talked about our futures. As wild and as beautiful. I can see any man could get lost in you."

Cora could have blushed. "You learned more than army skills in the service, didn't you?" She looked down. "If I was wild back then, I surely have become a little more tame now." Cora looked up again. "But I'm back here in St. Petersburg, and I've decided St. Pete is going to be my home until they burn this old body of mine and scatter my ashes."

"Now you sound like some of the old folks talking," Warren replied. "Except for I don't know too many who want to be cremated instead of buried."

"Do I?" Cora chuckled. "Maybe I feel like one."

They both laughed.

"You know something?" Warren cocked his head.

"What?"

"All those years we were around each other in school, you never realized I was in love with you."

"No-o." Cora tried to hold Warren's gaze, but she found herself looking away.

"Ye-es," Warren said. "Yes I was. Head over heels. Crazy about me some Cora."

They laughed again.

"But your head was too far in the clouds to see me. You were on your way to your life."

"Oh, Warren." Cora's brow creased. "Was I that mean?"

"You weren't mean, Cora. You were just yourself."

"Just selfish, huh?"

"Not selfish. Focused on knowing there was a bigger world out there and you were going to go and find it your way," Warren replied.

Cora nodded. "And it looks like you found it your way, too."

"I did." Warren's chin lifted. "I did a lot of traveling in the service. Seen all kinds of people in different countries, and it's been good for me. I feel like I grew there."

"I'd say you did. Literally." Cora rose on her toes attempting to see the top of his head.

Lucille came back with a wad of foil. She gave it to Cora.

"Thanks, Miss Lucille," Cora said. "And it was so good seeing you, Warren. How long you going to be here?"

"I'm not sure," Warren replied. "It depends on my finding a job. If I do, I'll be around."

"I'd love that," Lucille said. "You've been away so long I'd like to spend a little time with you. You know you can always stay here."

Warren put his arm around his mother's shoulder. "I know. And I might take you up on that for a couple of days until I can find something else. But I need to find out if St. Pete is going to welcome me." He looked at Cora.

"I hope it does," she replied.

Warren's gaze swept over her face before he nodded.

"Thanks again, Miss Lucille. But I guess I better go." Cora went to the door. Lucille followed and opened it.

"It was good seeing you, Warren." Cora stepped down onto the stoop.

"You, too."

The door closed and Cora walked, slowly, toward her mother's place. When she went inside, Cora gave Nebia the salt, as she gazed off into space.

"What happened to you back there?" Nebia took the foil.

"What?"

"You got this strange look about you now. Look at her, Laura."

"Yeah there's something going on, alright."

"Really?" Cora looked around. "The only thing different that I know of is Warren's back."

"Oh ye-es. Miss Lucille said her boy was coming home," Laura replied.

"He's anything but a boy now." Cora exhaled. "He's six feet three and dressed in a uniform. He was enough to take your breath away."

"Seems like he did." Laura's chin lowered. She cut her eyes toward Nebia.

Cora threw up her hands. "I shouldn't have said a word." Cora turned on her heels and reopened the door. "I'm going in the back to paint."

Nebia's Story . . .

"So, Warren and Cora made quite a connection," Erica remarked.

"I'd say so, but Cora wasn't about to talk about it," Nebia replied. "And so there was no way for Laura and I to really know what was swimming around in that head of hers. Cora just continued to busy herself with the things she wanted to do."

"And what was that?" Cynthia asked.

"Mostly painting and spending a lot of quiet time in the park. But then the time came when Cora decided painting over the garage and sitting in that park with those kids gathered 'round wasn't enough. So she opened up a business."

"Just like that?" Cynthia snapped her fingers. "What kind of business?"

Nebia stop rocking. "It was a combination of things. She called it The Way Home. Cora sold her paintings there, and some of her African imports." She started rocking again. "But she also opened it up to the children. Cora would let them paint, but only after they had meditated. Then she told them to paint what they saw or felt." Nebia chuckled. "She had those kids playing those instruments from Africa any kind of way they wanted. Yes, Cora turned out quite different from anybody else around here."

"I'd say so," Sheila replied. "That was really different back then."

"Around here it seemed to be. But there was quite a movement in this country with some black folks who were into their blackness, and looking for something else. A spiritual way."

"Looking for something else," Erica said. "But what about God? Did Cora believe in God? You're saying she had these kids meditating and all that, but did Cora ever bring God into the picture?" Erica crossed her arms.

"The thing about that, Erica, is sometimes people experience God in different ways. Cora saw God in nature. She saw having a good heart as God."

"I don't know about Cora." Erica looked off.

"And me either, huh?" Nebia smiled and looked down. "But you aren't the only person who wasn't so sure about Cora. She soon met opposition because of her unusual ways."

Chapter 21

Cora stood back and examined the newest addition to the vibrant wall of The Way Home. The bright peach backdrop was sprinkled with the paintings of the center's students. Cora wanted The Way Home to be a reflection of the children who came there. There was only one area that was not about the kids. It showcased some of Cora's paintings and a few African imports that were for sale.

"I'm going to put my painting right over here in this corner so nobody can mess with it," the girl said. "Last time somebody knocked it over and got it all messed up. I want this one to be perfect, so when I take it home my Mama will like it."

"It should be safe over there. We'll hang it on the wall tomorrow," Cora replied.

"Miss Cora?"

"Yes."

"Is this the way you started painting?"

"Oh no. Not at all," Cora said.

"Well, how *did* you get started, Miss Cora?" The girl pressed.

Cora raised an eyebrow. "It's a long story, Vernecia. And it's late, so you won't be hearing it tonight."

"But you will tell us?" Vernecia said with a pleading look.

"Maybe," Cora replied.

"Alright." She looked disappointed as she joined another girl by the door.

"But we want to know," a second girl insisted. "So we're going to keep asking you about it."

"I don't doubt that." Cora turned her back to put some sketch pads in the cupboard.

The door opened.

"Miss Cora! There's a policeman about to come in here," Vernecia announced.

"Let him in." She straightened the pads. "Policemen can paint too, I guess."

"But when do they find the time and the energy? That's what I'd like to know."

Cora turned around. It was Warren. "Hello-o," she said.

"Hello." He removed his cap.

"I see you've traded one uniform for another." Cora shook the brushes and laid them on a towel.

"I see you've traded one home for another," Warren replied. "The Way Home . . . this is yours?"

"It's mine," Cora said with pride.

Warren looked around. "You couldn't have been here very long."

Cora looked, too. "Is it so obvious?"

"No." Warren smiled. "I say that because this is my beat. And I've only been off for a couple of days and before I left there was no business in here."

Cora smiled too. "Oh-h. You're right. I got in here early Thursday and was busy, busy, busy through Friday evening. That's when I had my first session, which I'm happy to say was attended by a few kids from the neighborhood."

"So you've actually got kids interested in this?" He scanned the freshly painted paintings.

"I sure do." Cora stood straight and tall. "It's great, and I'm going to enjoy this very much."

Warren walked over to one of the paintings. "What do you tell them to paint?" He leaned forward.

"Whatever they see in their mind's eye. What they see after they've gone inside themselves. I tell them to paint what they see or what they feel."

"Sho 'nuff." Warren walked around and looked at a few more paintings. "Well, they sure are seeing and feeling a lot."

"Don't we all?" Cora replied. "When we let ourselves?"

Warren turned and looked at her. "I would say that's very true." Their gazes held.

"But how do you make a living from this, Cora?"

She inhaled. "Money isn't my goal, Warren. I'm not trying to make a fortune. I just want to help these kids know their strengths. And to know that being an individual is good. They don't have to follow the crowd."

He walked over and stood in front of her. "That's all well and good, Cora, but—uh, you do need to make money. It's just the way things are. You can't survive without it. You might be able to eat and sleep off Miss Laura for a little while, but—"

"I don't intend to live off of my mother for the rest of my life." Cora crossed her arms. "And I'll have you know I actually add to the family income. I make a little bit of money by selling my paintings." She pointed. "Every once in a while some wise, open person buys one. And I have things that come from Africa that sell okay." Her chin lifted. "As far as the kids go, sometimes there is a small fee to cover the supplies. And so far, so good."

"You think so?"

"Absolutely." Cora regained her footing from Warren's pointed question. "Now, what about you? You're a policeman?"

"Ye-es. I'm not wearing this uniform for fun."

Cora made a face. "How did you come up with that?"

Warren looked amused. "I came up with it because this is what I want to be. Policemen do have a purpose in this society, you know.

We're not all bad. We're not all pigs." He shrugged. "We look after people. We try to keep order, because life doesn't work well without it."

"I realize that." Cora backed down a bit. "I just never thought that one of my friends would be a policeman."

"So you consider me to be a friend?"

Cora relaxed on one hip. "Warren, you'll always be a friend."

"Huh." He spun the cap in his hand. "And there's no possibility for anything more?"

Cora got quiet. "I don't know. I hadn't really thought about it."

"Now that, Cora, is a lie," Warren replied.

Her mouth dropped open. "What? Did you just call me a liar?"

"I did. A beautiful liar, but a liar nevertheless."

"Your uniform is not a license to be rude. I—"

"So if you feel the need to lie to me, perhaps even to yourself right now," Warren continued, "it's okay. I'll let you slide for awhile. But I'm going to want the truth at some point, Cora."

He looked deep into her eyes as if he were searching for it.

Cora didn't know what to say.

"Have you eaten?" Warren went to safer grounds.

"No." Cora picked at her arm. "I was going to go home and see what I could scrounge up."

"No scrounging for you tonight," Warren replied. "I'm on lunch break. Would you like to go around the corner and sit down and have something to eat at what's going to be one of my favorite spots? It's called Atwaters."

Cora paused just a second. "Why not?" she replied.

Warren waited while Cora put everything away and locked up. Then they headed down the street together.

Nebia's Story . . .

"I told you, Miss Nebia, there was something going on between those two," Erica said. "And you said you weren't so sure about that."

"Of course I knew there was something," Nebia replied. "But I said Cora never talked about it. At least for a good while she didn't." Nebia licked her lips. "But yes, I saw it in her face the day she saw Warren for the first time after he returned to St. Petersburg."

"And her feelings were so strong that you saw them, but Cora was still having a hard time admitting anything," Cynthia added.

"No doubt she was." Nebia swiped at a mosquito. "I don't think Cora knew what to do with those kinds of feelings. She had known what to do with attraction, lust, but not feelings that had more permanent rumblings. And Warren realized Cora's predicament," Nebia continued. "So he took it slow. It was because he knew her as a child. He knew Cora's roots, what made her who she was. Warren really knew Cora, so when she tried to pretend as if there was nothing there, he told her it was fine. He gave her time to be in that comfortable space. But he also warned her that she was going to have to come out of there. To come out and meet him in a love that was adult. That deserved a commitment." Nebia paused. "Because Warren knew Cora wanted it."

"And did he ask her?" Erica asked.

"When the time was right . . . yes, Warren did. And Cora was ready."

Chapter 22

"Well, I've got you now." Cora smiled and turned her body toward Warren as she sat in the passenger seat.

"You think so?" Warren glanced at her, then returned his gaze to the road as he continued to drive.

She nodded slowly. "I most certainly do. Because I've never seen you dance before, Warren. Never. Never. Never. Not while we were in high school. None of the time when we'd get together in the backyard and show what we could do. You'd just sit and watch. You'd never join in. And now"—she counted on her fingers—"we've been out one, two, three . . . we've been out four times. You've taken me to eat, we've been to the movies, but every time I said, 'let's go out so we can dance,' you'd say something like, 'don't want to do that.' So I just figured it was because you can't."

"And that's what you get for figuring," Warren replied. "Because here we are, on our way."

"Yeah." Cora chuckled. "And that's how I know I've got you. I've pressured you so much that you finally gave in with your no-dancing self." She chuckled again. "So this is going to be interesting."

"It sure is." Warren nodded.

Cora studied his profile, and she knew there wasn't a woman alive who wouldn't think Warren was a good-looking man. Every time the lights from the oncoming cars flashed inside their vehicle, in Cora's mind Warren shone like a gem. She couldn't tear her eyes away. She took in everything down to the length of his eyelashes.

Warren glanced at her. "What's gotten into you?"

Cora looked down. "Nothing. Can't a woman be quiet if she wants to?"

"Not you. You're always talking."

"See there." Cora turned her body toward the dashboard and folded her hands in her lap. "You think you know everything about me. Well, you don't." She looked out the window, but in her mind's eye Cora was seeing every detail of Warren's face. Especially his mouth. He had never kissed her. Not really.

"Have you been to CeCe's before?" Warren asked.

"No, I've never been," Cora replied. "But I've heard some pretty good things about it. I heard some of the kids talking about their folks going there and loving it. But I've also heard them whispering among themselves. They talk about who got drunk at CeCe's, and who got caught with somebody else."

"I heard a few things about it myself," Warren replied. "We made an arrest over there one night, but overall it's a pretty good place. I hear it's got great food, and CeCe's kitchen is open half the night. So, it's been doing pretty good. Hear it's got a good D.J. and all, so we should have a pretty good time."

They drove for another five minutes before they pulled up in front of CeCe's. It was simply a house stuck in the middle of a row of what were obviously businesses. There were cars parked all up and down the street.

Warren and Cora parked and got out. They walked toward the building. When they stepped inside Cora noticed how the living room had been converted to a dance floor, and the dining room was the dining area with small tables and chairs. The tables were topped with crocheted tablecloths. Glass soda bottles served as candleholders, and what had been a large pantry was now the

D.J.'s booth. His records were stacked and labeled on the shelves around him.

A healthy woman wearing a dress that fit every one of her curves walked over with a smile that was as inviting as the music.

"I'm CeCe. Welcome." She stretched out her hand.

"Hi, CeCe," Cora replied.

"Good to meet you," Warren said.

"I don't know if you know it, but we are a restaurant with a dance floor. Are you planning to eat?" The question separated the paying customers from the loiterers.

"Yes, we are expecting to have dinner," Warren replied.

"Good," CeCe said. "And I've got just the table for you." She picked up a menu that had been handwritten and directed them toward a corner table. "Come with me."

Cora and Warren followed her and sat down.

"Donna will be over to take your order in a minute. I hope you enjoy yourselves." CeCe smiled again.

"From what I can see," Cora replied, "I'm sure we will."

They looked over the menu as the D.J. played an old blues tune that had several people jumping and moving on the dance floor. Cora laughed at the antics of one man. "I think there's going to be some performances up in here tonight," Cora said.

Warren glanced at the dance floor. "Do you plan to join them?"

"Yes, *we* do plan to join them."

"I'm not talking about just dancing," Warren said. "I'm talking about acting a fool like that fellow out there."

Cora laughed. "I might do a little of that, too. You know who you've got over here, Warren Gray."

"Yeah, I know who you think you are, and who you've been determined to be up to this point in your life. People don't always remain the same, Cora. As time passes, people change."

"Most people do, I guess. I can't say I haven't made some changes," Cora replied. "I have, as a matter of fact."

"I know you have. That's why I'm saying what I'm saying right now."

She looked in his eyes. They were so serious and dark. Cora looked down at the menu. "See, you starting in too serious too fast for me. And I'm too hungry for that. I'm going to pick what I'm going to eat."

"Please do. I'm just making conversation." Warren smiled.

Minutes later Donna arrived. "Are you ready to order?"

"I am," Cora replied.

"Go right ahead." Donna readied her pad and pencil.

"I'll have your green beans, your greens, and some of this macaroni and cheese. And I want some cornbread with that."

"All right. What kind of meat are you having?"

"No meat for me," Cora replied.

Donna, who was obviously a teenager, made a funny face. "And you, sir?"

"Let's see, I think I'm going to have this, CeCe's Killer Smothered Chicken."

"All right."

"And give me a side of your lima beans, and—uh, I'll take some corn."

"Anything to drink?" Donna looked from Warren to Cora.

"You have tea, don't you?" Cora looked at the menu again.

"Yes, we have sweet tea."

"I'll take some sweet tea."

"Start me off with some tea, too," Warren said.

"I'll bring your drinks out in a minute," Donna replied before she walked away.

The drinks came and the food followed shortly after, and Cora and Warren engaged in conversation about the restaurant, CeCe, Laura, and life in general. The conversation flowed easily—the talk of two people who had known each other for a lifetime. The talk of friends.

Once the meal was done, Cora sat back and took a deep breath.

"My goodness, and when I first ordered I promised myself dessert, apple pie with vanilla ice cream on top. But now I can't eat another thing."

"This hit the spot for me," Warren replied. "I'm feeling just fine. Not too much, not too little."

The song in the background ended and the dancers began to return to their tables.

Donna popped up again. "Can I get you something else?"

"You can bring me a beer," Warren said.

She looked at Cora.

"I'll have some more iced tea," Cora replied. Donna picked up Cora's glass and walked away.

"When a Man Loves a Woman" began to play. Cora watched a couple get up and go to the dance floor. She looked across the table and saw Warren rise from his chair as well. He came and stood in front of her and stretched out his hand. Cora looked at it.

"It's time," Warren said.

"Time for what?" Cora challenged.

"You'll see once we get out there."

She looked into his eyes, then said, "All right."

Cora placed her hand in Warren's and followed him on to the floor. When they stopped, Warren pulled Cora to him and wrapped his arms around her. It was uncanny how her head fit so neatly just below his shoulder. Cora couldn't help but close her eyes at the feel of him. They had been going places together for a couple of months, but all that time Warren had kept his distance. At first Cora didn't know what to think about it, but she finally concluded Warren just wanted to be friends. But now, as he held her in his arms, the feeling that came over her made Cora know that, for her, it was more than friendship.

Warren began to move in a simple but rhythmic fashion as they held each other in silence, and the music and the lyrics washed over them.

"The D.J. couldn't have picked a better song, Cora," Warren finally whispered.

Her brows knitted. "Really?"

"I think he's playing it just for us."

Cora's heart beat a little faster as she continued to lie against his chest. "What are you talking about?"

"This is how I feel about you," Warren said as he pressed Cora against him. "I've fallen hard for you, Cora. I had to really search inside myself and see if what I was feeling was the real thing . . . but I really knew it from the moment I saw you come into my mother's house to get that salt. I knew I still loved you, that I had loved you all my life as I told you even then."

Cora felt like she was melting. It was an unexpected, disconcerting feeling, and she tried to play it down. "Warren, you think you love me." She looked up at him with a teasing smile. "We've been friends so long, you can't tell friendship from love."

"Yes, I can. I know what love is." He looked into her eyes. "And so do you."

"What do you mean, so do I?"

"Just what I said. I can feel it right now as I'm holding you," Warren replied. "There's no way you don't feel it, too. If it's this strong for me, you've got to feel something."

Cora's brow lifted. "I feel it all right. But what I'm feeling, I don't know if it's love or not. I haven't been in a man's arms in a long time. And I'm not the kind of woman who's been accustomed to doing without. I've got needs, Warren." She paused. "You've been taking me to eat and to movies and everything. And we've all got needs. I think, maybe you and I . . . it's time for us to fill that space for one another."

"There's no doubt in my mind, Cora, that we could fill each other's needs, but I'm talking about more than that. I can fill my needs with some of anybody. Sex is such a base thing. Something even dogs can do. I'm not talking about that. I'm talking about love, commitment. I'm talking about marriage."

Cora's feet felt as if they had stuck to the floor. "Marriage?"

"That's right. Marriage," Warren continued. "You and me. We know each other, Cora. We've known each other all our lives so there's no need to get to know each other any better. And these couple of months that we've been spending time together have shown me who you are as an adult woman, and I hope I have shown you who I am as a man. So I don't want to play no game of hit it and quit it, Cora. Let's see how it fits." Warren paused. "This is the real thing. I'm talking about our lives, and I'm talking about our future. I want you to marry me, Cora."

"Warren, I never thought about marrying anybody," she replied. "It's just not been who I am."

"It's not been who you decided you were as a young girl, and it may not have been who you decided you were when you left home, but life is unpredictable, Cora. You know you are one of the last people that I have to tell that to." He paused again. "We have to mold our happiness in the way we want it. We shouldn't set our-selves up for failure as two people who come together playing with each other, having no sense of commitment. I don't want to play that game, Cora. It's not the game for me to play. Not with you it isn't. You say you haven't thought about marriage, while I'm giving you an opportunity to think about it."

Cora put her face to his chest again. "I'll think about it."

"I hope you will. You think about it right now while we're on this dance floor." Cora stiffened and Warren continued. "I don't want you to tell me your answer when we get over there to that table. I don't want your answer in a couple weeks when we've thought about making love over and over again, thought about how it will feel, thought about it so much it has almost driven us insane. By then our desire for one another will be so strong we won't even be able to think about what I've said here. Cora . . ."

"Yes?"

"I want you to tell me your answer once this dance is done. You're either going to be my wife or you're not. I've waited long enough."

They continued to dance in silence as Warren's hold on Cora tightened, and her embrace tightened as well, while their fate was being decided by the length of a song. When Percy Sledge sang the last sentence of the tune, Cora and Warren stopped dancing and held one another.

Cora heard Warren ask, "What's your answer? I got to know. I've got to know now."

Cora looked up at his face, and deep into the eyes that held a lifelong friendship, a lifelong love. It took only a moment for Cora to reply, "Yes, I'll marry you, Warren."

Then right there in the middle of the dance floor while everyone in the room looked on, Warren and Cora sealed their future with a kiss.

Nebia's Story . . .

"Now I like a man like that. A man that knows what he wants and he goes right for it. Warren said don't dance around me and try to tell me this that and the other. I want you, and either you want me or you don't." Cynthia slapped her thigh. "Find me a man like that."

Erica and Sheila laughed.

"What can you say?" Sheila said. "There they were, and Cora knew she wasn't going to let Warren get away. She loved him."

"Yeah, I think she did," Erica replied.

"Yes, she loved him and it was beautiful," Nebia said. "Because I tell you, from that day until their wedding day, Cora had a glow that could light the world. It was like she had been born again, and it just spilled out on all of us." Nebia looked down. "At least most of us, that is."

Chapter 23

Dressed in one of her finest outfits, Brenda watched Michael get out of his car and approach the house. She opened the door. There was a tinge of irritation on her face. "You better hurry up or we're going to be late."

"Late?" Michael closed the door. "Late for what?" He looked at her.

"Late for the wedding," Brenda replied.

Michael squinted.

"The wedding, Michael. Cora and Warren's wedding."

"They are getting married?" Disbelief hung with the question.

Brenda held her breath. "Yes. I told you about the invitation over a month ago."

"But I just thought . . ." He looked through the window. "I guess I didn't believe that—that they would do it. That Cora would actually marry."

Brenda looked away, then walked further into the house. "Well, you were wrong."

Michael clenched his eyes and held them shut.

"She's getting married in an hour, and if we're going to be there you better hurry."

Michael changed clothes and met Brenda, who was waiting quietly in the front room. "I'm ready."

She rose from the couch and started toward the door. Michael stopped her. He pulled her to him. It was a short uncomfortable embrace. Eventually, they made their way outside and climbed inside the car. Michael started the ignition. "I didn't realize you and Cora talked."

"We don't really," Brenda replied. "I've bumped into her accidentally on a couple of occasions. But since that first evening when she came by, we haven't really gotten together. The invitation came in the mail along with a special note, saying that it would break her heart if I wasn't there. If I didn't come to her wedding."

Michael's hands tightened on the steering wheel. "Of course it would. You're her sister," he said softly.

"But the invitation was to both of us." She looked at his hardened profile. "She wanted you to be there too, Michael."

He nodded. "So where is it being held?"

"At Mama's house. In the backyard." Then she added in a hushed whisper, "Where this all started."

Michael glanced at Brenda but he remained quiet as he drove.

They were both surprised by the number of cars that lined the street, and the number of people who had crowded into the Robinsons' small backyard. Several of Cora's students served as ushers and one quickly directed Brenda and Michael to a couple of chairs near the front, almost directly behind Laura and Nebia. Lucille sat across the aisle from Laura, a lone white face in a sea of blackness. Brenda edged forward and was about to touch her mother's shoulder when the wedding music began.

It was not your traditional wedding march, and Cora did not walk down the aisle to meet a waiting Warren. They walked the aisle together and Warren held a decorated broom between them as he advanced in a tailored suit. Cora, on the other hand, wore a dress of layered gauze, the color of maize. Cora's slightest movement gave it life. A matching scarf covered her head and face, while the ends floated behind her.

Cora and Warren stopped in the front of their guests and without a minister they began their vows.

"I stand here before you, Cora Robinson, one of the happiest men in the world. This moment has been a dream of mine ever since I was a boy, and now standing here before you, offering myself as a man, I know the fullness of this moment will never leave me. For me you are all a woman, a wife, a mother should be. You are the fulfillment of my dreams, and the seed for my future. I am filled with joy and pride because you have agreed to be my wife." Warren reached into his pocket. "And I place this ring on your finger as a constant reminder of what you are to me, and what we will be together. One." Warren lifted Cora's hand and placed the ring on her finger.

For a prolonged moment Cora stared at it before she lifted her eyes to Warren's.

"Warren Gray," Cora began, "a name and a face that I have known almost all my life. I never guessed that you would be the man to bring me to this place. A place of surrender. Of love. Of hopes, and of understanding that loving one man, truly loving him, can be more fulfilling than a lifetime of experiences. I love you, Warren. I am so glad to say that, to share that with you, and those who have gathered here." She looked at the sky. "I look forward to our life together." Her chin lowered and her eyes were on Warren again. "And I hope to be as good of a wife and mother as I know you will be a husband and father. All I ask is that you have patience with me if I lose my way, and know that within my heart this love for you will always lead me back to the right road, my union with you, my marriage." Cora slipped a ring onto Warren's hand, and with mutual eagerness they came together in a kiss. Afterwards Cora and Warren turned to the crowd. Two of the ushers picked up the waiting broom and laid it on the grass in front of them.

With huge smiles they jumped the broom together and declared, "We are now husband and wife." Applause erupted and nearly drowned out their last words, "Warren and Cora Gray."

Lucille was one of the first to get up. She came forward and hugged her son and her new daughter-in-law. But when Cora was able, she broke away and came over to Laura, who continued to sit by a standing Nebia. Cora gave Nebia a peck on the cheek before she bent over and hugged and kissed her mother. In return, Laura held her so tight it was obvious for all eyes to see.

Cora loosened the embrace as her eyes met Brenda's, then Michael's.

"Congratulations, Cora," Brenda said softly.

Cora leaned forward and placed her cheek against her sister's. "Thank you."

Michael continued to focus on Cora's face. His eyes reflected his turmoil. "I guess I thought you'd never do it," Michael said stiffly. "But here you are. Congratulations."

"Thank you," Cora replied. An uncertain moment followed where Cora started to hug Michael, but she reached out her hands and held his hand in hers instead. Moments later Cora was back at Warren's side where a crowd descended on them.

After a long line of congratulations, Cora and Warren encouraged their guests to start on the food. Three picnic tables placed side by side were covered with white table cloths and several dishes and desserts. The music began and things were just getting started when Brenda and Michael left without saying good-bye. But that did not mar the celebration that went on for hours into the night.

Nebia's Story . . .

"So Michael just couldn't take it," Sheila said. "He had to make Brenda leave early."

"No, it wasn't just Michael," Nebia replied. "It was Brenda, too. How Michael felt was written all over his face, but I could also see how uncomfortable Brenda was. She was uncomfortable there. How else could it be? There was too much water under the bridge. And so Brenda and Michael came and did their duty. They showed their faces and slipped off as soon as they could. But even with everything that was going on, I saw how Cora watched them leave."

"Did she look upset?" Erica asked.

"I wouldn't say that. But I felt a little sadness. Maybe it was because of her distant relationship with Brenda. Or it could have been because Michael's pain over her marrying another man was so clear." Nebia coughed. "Either way, you know what Cora did?"

They shook their heads, and someone said, "No."

"She deliberately turned to her new husband and kissed him. Kissed him hard. She was determined to make the best of her life. That's what Cora did."

Chapter 24

Brenda looked at Pastor Benson's Cadillac before she descended the stairs to the church basement. She met two young men on the stairwell. "Hello," she said. "How are you all doing this evening?

"Doin' fine."

"Is the tutoring going okay?"

One of them shrugged. The other replied, "Yeah, I'm sort of getting the hang of it."

"Good." She smiled. "We'll see you Friday."

They nodded and continued up the stairs.

Brenda turned into the small hallway where several coats and hats hung on hooks. A woman and a young girl entered the walk-through closet and began to put on their coats.

"Hi, Mrs. Dawson," the woman said.

"Hello," Brenda replied. "How are you this evening?"

"I'm okay." The woman glanced at the girl. "I guess."

Brenda focused on the girl, who wore a sour look on her face. "Is everything okay?" she asked.

The girl shrugged and her mother jabbed her with her elbow.

"Don't shrug at her. She's your elder. You speak up when Mrs. Dawson is asking you something."

"It's okay," the girl replied softly.

"Is the tutoring helping with school?" Brenda attempted to engage the girl further.

"A little bit."

"Good." She glanced at the mother, then back at the girl. "Then you should be happy."

"She's not happy because she wants to be where her friends are," the mother replied.

"And where is that?"

"In that place your sister's opened up. The Way Home. She says all of her friends are going there."

"They do." The girl piped up. "And they learn to paint. And they do this thing called meditation where they use their minds to just see things that's in 'em."

"Well, you're not going there." The mother's face hardened. "I don't care if you weren't going to the tutorial program. Ain't no child of mine going there. Do you hear me?"

"Yes ma'am." The girl looked down.

The woman looked at Brenda. "I don't mean to be harsh or anything, but I'm going to be honest with you, and I'm not alone in this. I just don't like what's going on at your sister's place. This meditating and all. Painting what you see, and God talking to you directly. How they know that's God talking to them? How they know that? That's her saying that. It could be Satan for all we know."

"I would doubt that." Brenda shook her head.

"Well you doubt it because it's your sister. But some of us, including the pastor, aren't so certain."

"What has Pastor Benson said about Cora?"

The woman lifted her chin. "Let me put it this way. When she got married and that's been over a year now, from the very beginning, it was obvious to many of us that she don't honor God too well. She didn't even have a minister perform the ceremony. I heard she stood up there on her own, she and that policeman husband of hers, saying what they wanted to say to each other. Who ever heard of such a thing?"

"Well . . . Ms. . . . what's your name?"

"Ms. Steele. Velma Steele."

"Well Ms. Steele, if you had been there I think you might have a different opinion. What Cora and Warren said to each other was very loving, and positive."

"I'm not talking about what it seems like on the outside. I'm talking about the way it was done. And anybody who gets married without God sanctioning their wedding, I got a problem with it. A few of us do, and I don't think they should be teaching our children ways that are more satanic than godly. Pastor Benson agrees with us, at least that's my understanding." She cleared her throat. "But I can't speak for him. Maybe you need to ask him yourself." Velma pulled her hat down on her head. "Well, we're going to get on out of here. I just . . ." Velma looked down. "You asked me what was happening with her"—she gave her daughter a gentle shove forward—"and I told you. You probably need to know anyway because there's quite a bit of talk about it around the neighborhood."

"Really?" Brenda replied.

"Yes. Really," Velma replied as she walked away. "Thank you, though, for letting my daughter be in this program. She is doing better in school even if she don't want to admit it. And we shall see you on Friday."

"All right."

Brenda went to the bathroom. Then, before she knew it, she was climbing another set of stairs. They ended at a back hallway that led to the pastor's office. Brenda walked past the baptismal pool and stopped in front of the pastor's door, which was closed. She rapped on the door. A few moments later it opened slightly.

"Pastor Benson, I'd like to speak with you, if you have time."

He hesitated. "Sure, I've got a moment. I think we're finished in here."

Pastor Benson looked back. Indistinguishable words followed before the pastor opened the door completely. Two young men very closely associated with the Gangster Disciples, the largest gang in the neighborhood, walked past them.

"Good evening," one of them said.

"Good evening," Brenda replied.

"Catch you later, Pastor Benson," the other said.

"Good-bye." The remark was sharp. Pastor Benson motioned for Brenda to step inside. He closed the door. "Have a seat."

Brenda sat down. "Aren't those two young men members of the Gangster Disciples?"

"Yes. Yes, they are." Pastor Benson sat back in his chair. "I've been trying to counsel them. Show them a different way."

"Is it doing any good?" Brenda placed her hands in her lap. "I'm so surprised to see them here. I've never seen them in church."

Pastor Benson massaged his chin. "It might take a little time, but it can't hurt. The world wasn't made in a day, you know." He placed folded hands on his desk. "Now, Brenda, what can I help you with?"

"Well—" she looked down, then started again. "One of the parents, Velma Steele, was picking her daughter up from tutoring, and she told me that she along with some other parents, and you, seem to have a problem with my sister Cora and her business."

"Oh, I see," Pastor Benson replied. "Well, the truth is, some of the parents have come to me confidentially and spoken of their concerns about your sister. She seems to have captured the attention, and even the hearts, of quite a few of the young folks in the community, and the parents just aren't so sure if her way is the way they want their children to take on. They feel that—uh . . . the things she does are a little foreign and that makes them uncomfortable. Even frightens some of them."

"And what do you say to them, Pastor?"

"I have my feelings, too." He sat back. "I'm not pleased that—uh, she's not seeking out the ministry here, seeking out the church, even with your being her sister and your involvement. I believe if your sister brought prayer into the situation, instead of this meditating, we would all feel more comfortable." Pastor Benson sat forward with a pastoral smile. "I'm just afraid that she is functioning without a capable intermediary of God's in all of this."

"I'm sure Cora doesn't feel she needs an intermediary, Pastor. Cora feels if God talks to you, He'll talk to her, and He'll talk to those children, too," Brenda replied. "No one's special in the eyes of God. She believes if you open your heart to God, God will be there."

"I see you seem to support this uncertain road that your sister is traveling."

"It's not a matter of supporting it, Pastor. Cora is a person who has always been a seeker of a different kind, and I've learned, being her older sister, to let her be. And I've learned to try to let others be as well, as long as their intentions are good."

"What about all these children that are flocking to her? Wanting to take on her ways? I'm telling you now, Brenda, I just don't think it's good."

"Have you heard of something she's done that's hurt somebody? Something specific?"

"Not yet. But—uh, we don't want it to get there." He sat up straight. "We'd like to nip it in the bud before somebody gets hurt."

"I see." Brenda crossed her arms.

"And I'm not just talking about the children, I'm talking about your sister, too."

"What do you mean?" Brenda's brow furrowed.

"I heard that some of the gang members had been giving her trouble. Threatening her even. It seems they're not too happy because some of the boys that used to show an interest in becoming gang members are now going to your sister's place. I just had a talk about it with those young men who were in here."

"Well, that shows some good that's coming out of what Cora is doing, right there," Brenda replied. "If she can discourage our young men from fighting one another and committing crimes, you'd think the neighborhood would be behind her."

Pastor Benson pressed his lips together. "If only it was that simple, Brenda. Look"—the pastor leaned on his desk—"maybe you should talk to her about what people are saying. Try to convince her that she needs to be a part of the church community."

"Pastor"—Brenda shook her head—"that's not going to happen."

A look of irritation flitted across his face. "What's not going to happen? Which part? Your talking to her?" He gave her the eye. "Or her becoming a part of the church community?"

"I guess my sister and I have been the topic of many conversations." Brenda stood up. "If you want Cora to stop doing what she's doing, you talk to her. Because from where I stand, she's not doing any harm. Good night, Pastor Benson." She left his office.

Nebia's Story . . .

"Cora was stirring stuff up," Cynthia said.

"She was beginning to," Nebia replied. "But I don't think Cora knew how much. Sure, once in a while she complained about some of the young thugs in the neighborhood banging on The Way Home's door and shouting she was taking their members. But I don't think Cora had an inkling that the church community was becoming upset with her. She was too busy in her own world to know. Her business was growing and she and Warren had bought a little house. Cora was happy making a life for herself." Nebia looked at each one of them. "The kind of life she never dreamed of having, but when she got it, it was more than she had hoped for."

"Did Brenda talk to Cora about what was being said?" Erica asked.

"I don't think so," Nebia replied. "I think Brenda truly didn't feel Cora was doing any harm, and if she couldn't go to her sister with something loving to say, I think Brenda decided not to go to her at all. And when she told that pastor that he should go talk to her, she meant just that." Nebia lit another cigarette. "So Cora just kept on her merry way. More and more young people started going to The Way Home, and she sold more paintings. There was even a need to stock more African items to sell."

"Who was buying them?" Cynthia remained skeptical. "I wouldn't think the folks in the neighborhood would be interested."

"They weren't. But folks passing through town and people from the surrounding areas, like Tampa and Sarasota, bought them. Yes, even some of the white folks from Sarasota were interested in her imports. Cora was doing well." Nebia blew a long stream of smoke. "And Laura was proud. She was proud of both of her girls actually, even though she never said it. I would see a light come in her eye when she'd read about Brenda in the *Sentinel*, one of our black newspapers. Brenda and Michael were always in there doing something or 'nother. And I could tell Laura was proud and happy that both of her daughters seemed settled. But because of that 'thing' between she and Brenda, Laura poured all of her emotion out on Cora."

Chapter 25

"Sometimes I just shouldn't let her have her way, Miss Laura. I just shouldn't." Warren paced the Robinsons' small living room.

"I know how you feel. Cora can be extremely headstrong." Laura looked concerned. "No matter what you do or say, she got to do it her way."

"God." Warren stared at the ceiling. "Have I come to know that."

"Aa-a-argh!!!" erupted from the bedroom upstairs.

"I can't stand another moment of this." He held his head. "I'm going up there. I've got to go up there and tell them she needs a doctor."

Warren mounted the steps two at a time and opened the bedroom door. He saw Cora sitting on the bed holding her huge abdomen. Her teeth were bared, and her eyes were shut so tight, water ran from the corners. Cora didn't look at him; she was deep into her labor pains.

Nebia went over and mopped Cora's brow with a cool cloth, then she gently patted her face. When the contraction ended, Cora's hands dropped like limp noodles onto the bed. Warren went to her side.

"Cora, I can't stand this any longer. I just can't," he pleaded. "We need to get you to the hospital, and to a doctor. I want you to throw out this outdated idea of having our baby here. I—"

"Warren, we've talked about this a hundred—"

"I'm afraid for you, Cora." Warren took her face in both hands. "I'm afraid for you and the baby. I don't want anything to happen to you."

Cora took hold of his wrists. "Nothing's going to happen, Warren, except I'm going to have this child." Determination entered her voice. "And I'm going to have it here at this house."

Warren turned to Nebia. "Miss Nebia. Ple-ease. Tell her to come with me. Tell her to let me take her to the hospital. She's been going at this now for seven hours. Going at it hard, and I just can't stand it. I can't stand hearing her cry out."

"Son," Nebia said as she placed her hand on his back, "it's Cora's decision. She's asked me to help her have the baby here, and that's what I'm going to do. If she changes her mind, I'm with her as well."

"Maybe you should go and have a beer, or a drink." Cora tried to console him. "Just get out of the house for a while. You've been running up and down those stairs since I went into labor. You're going to wear yourself out." She smiled as sweat beaded her brow. "I'm the one in labor, but you're working just as hard as I am."

"Is everything all right up there?" Laura called from downstairs.

"It's fine, Mama. Warren's coming back down there with you. Tell him to get out of here."

"Okay." Warren squeezed his forehead. "All right." He leaned forward to kiss Cora's cheek, but her face mashed into a deep grimace.

"This is another one. And it's stronger than any of the rest." Cora's grip on Warren's wrist was intense. "Maybe you shouldn't go. Maybe you should wait downstairs just a little longer." She took hold of the bed.

Nebia shoved him, gently. "Go. Go downstairs. Go."

Warren stared at Cora as he went to the bedroom door. Reluctantly, he closed it behind him.

"You say this one is harder than the rest?"

"Uh-h . . . uh-h . . ." Cora's body heaved. "Yes."

"I got to check you again." Nebia grabbed a nearby towel and dabbed at Cora's face. "Ease back on the bed and let me see."

Weak, Cora scooted back and put her feet on the edge of the mattress. Nebia lifted the wide nightgown. "You're right, Cora. You're right. It's just about time, and I don't think it will be much longer," Nebia said. "It's time to get ready."

Nebia helped Cora stand. "Come on over here and take hold of the bedroom doorknob and the closet knob as I showed you."

On the other side of the contraction, Cora did as she was told but her head weaved from side to side from the depth of it.

"Now, when another pain hits you, squeeze those knobs," Nebia said. "Squeeze as hard as you need to. And whatever you do, push when I say so."

They looked at each other as Cora held on to the knobs with her knees flexed.

"The next time the contraction comes," Nebia repeated, "I want you to squeeze the knobs and I want you to squat and push with all"—Nebia gritted her teeth—"you got."

Cora nodded. She took several deep breaths, but when she looked into Nebia's eyes, Cora's eyes held fear.

"This is not the moment, child, to be afraid. This is the moment to gather all your strength and do what must be done."

Cora nodded again. "You're right. You're right." She panted. "And I've seen it done before. I've seen a woman in Zambia crouch down, there was a mound of soft hay beneath her, and while she held on to this stick that two of the women were holding, she bore down and pushed the baby out. I saw her do it, and if she could do it . . . if . . . she could . . . do it"—Cora gasped as another contraction mounted—"so-so can I. Uh! Uh!" She squatted fully and a sound emerged from deep within her body, a massive noise that in and of itself seemed to emit pressure.

"Push!" Nebia ordered. Cora grunted and pushed.

Nimble and quick, Nebia got on her knees. She extended her arms that were wrapped in a white towel, beneath Cora's body. Nebia waited for the baby to emerge. It was only a matter of moments before the child made her debut, quickly and smoothly, as if she could not wait any longer.

There was no need to shake her. There was no need to make her cry. She cried out loud and clear as she went into Nebia's waiting arms.

"Oh my God!" Cora looked down. "Oh God!" Cora exclaimed as she looked down at her freshly born child. "It's a girl, Nebia."

"Yes. It's a girl." Nebia smiled. "And the Robinsons' way continues." Quickly she cut the cord and tied it off. Then Nebia wrapped the baby inside the soft, downy towel.

"Look! Look-a-here." Cora reached for the baby, but her face contorted again. "It's another contraction." She grabbed the door-knobs again.

"It's the sack." Nebia declared, and no sooner than she said the words, the afterbirth emerged and Warren was at the door.

"Can I come in? Can I come in now?"

"One second," Nebia replied.

With effort, Cora wrapped the wide nightgown through and around her legs, turning them into pants before she made her way to the bed. Then Nebia placed the newborn child in Cora's arms.

She looked down and smiled. "Come in, Warren. Come in and see our beautiful baby."

The door swung open as Cora continued to gaze into the baby's face. Gently, she wiped it clean with a small cloth Nebia gave her. "It's a girl, Warren." She looked up. "We've got a baby girl."

"I can't believe it," Warren said, kneeling beside the bed. "She's so beautiful."

"She is, isn't she?" Cora replied.

"And so are you." Warren moved Cora's sweat-soaked locks out of her face.

"We're a family now," Cora said. "You. Me. And this little one."

Warren kissed the baby's forehead.

"Is everything all right up there?" Laura called.

"Yes, Mama. You've got a grandbaby. A little girl." Cora attempted to shout but her voice was weak. She handed the child to Warren. "Take her downstairs so Mama can see her."

Hesitantly, Warren reached out and Cora placed the little bundle in his arms.

"But hurry and bring her back."

"I've got to call my mother at work and let her know she's got a grandchild." Warren walked, slowly, carefully toward the bedroom door.

"Nebia." Cora reached out. "Come here."

Nebia crossed the floor and Cora took hold of her hand. She lifted it to her face. Tears wet the brown skin. "Nebia, you have always been here for me. And now you were here for me and my baby. I'll always be grateful to you, Nebia. All of my life, I will always be grateful."

"Hush, child. There is no need for all this. You're just emotional because you just gave birth."

"I did, didn't I? I just had a little girl." Cora cried and smiled. "I'm a mother, Nebia."

"Yes, you are." She tried to look stern but her eyes twinkled. "And God help the poor little thing having a mother like you."

Nebia's Story . . .

"Why wasn't Miss Laura in the room?" Sheila asked.

"By then Laura's condition had gotten worse," Nebia said. "Climbing the stairs just became too much for her. We actually had to turn the sun porch behind the kitchen into a bedroom."

"And mercy!" Cynthia grabbed her throat. "Cora actually had the baby holding on to two doorknobs?"

"Yes, she did. Ye-es she did," Nebia replied.

"I don't think I could do that." Erica frowned.

"I don't think you could either," Cynthia said. "You're scared to have a baby with an epidural and any other kind of 'dural that might help with the pain. So I know you wouldn't have one without any kind of anesthesia, holding on to two doorknobs."

"Like you would," Erica retorted.

Cynthia looked down. "You got a point there."

"Well, Cora did. And her baby was healthy and she was healthy," Nebia said. "And boy, was Warren one happy father. I don't know if I've ever seen a man that happy. And Laura"—Nebia shook her head—"when I went downstairs to get some special tea I'd been brewing for Cora . . . Laura was holding that baby and crying."

"I hear there's nothing like the first grandchild," Sheila said.

"If you judge the truth of that by Laura, I'd say you are absolutely right."

Chapter 26

"Brenda," Michael called. "Have you seen my navy blue pants with the cuffs?"

"Yes." She walked to the entrance of Michael's walk-in closet.

"Where are they?" Michael shuffled through several pants and jackets.

"They're at the cleaners."

"The cleaners?" He looked at her.

"I put them in the cleaners with the last batch of clothes."

"Oh-h." He shrugged. "It doesn't matter. I'll just wear these." He peeled a pair of brown slacks off of a hanger. "I did what I could to temporarily fix the situation with the water heater, but I think we'll need to get a professional in on Monday since it's too late now and tomorrow's Sunday." He slid one leg into his pants. Drops of water from his wet hair darkened the tan material in tiny splotches.

"Where are you going?"

"I've got a potential client that I'm going to talk to tonight. He's a white guy that owns a small business. He's got about fifty employ-

ees and should I be able to bring him aboard with an insurance
package, it'll open up the white market for me. At least that's my
strategy. How about you? What are you planning tonight?" Michael
continued to dress.

Brenda crossed her arms. "I thought that we had decided that
we'd have a nice quiet dinner together tonight." She walked
over in her most sultry fashion and put her arms around his
neck.

Michael stopped zipping his pants, but held onto the waistline.
"That sounds nice, but not tonight."

"Not tonight," she repeated softly, and kept her arms around his
neck.

They looked into each other's eyes.

"Not tonight," Brenda repeated. "That's suppose to be my line,
Michael, not yours." Her arms dropped to her sides. "I don't like
this. I don't like this at all." She shook her head. "Can you really
call this a marriage?"

Michael closed his eyes. "Yes, I do because I'm giving all I've
got to give here." He opened them. "Could it be better? Yes. But
it is a marriage, Brenda. We've got a beautiful home together.
We're respected in the community. Our futures are bright.
We—"

"What about the love, Michael? What about love?" Brenda stopped
him.

He looked down and buttoned the single button at the top of
his slacks. Then he said with resignation, "I love you, Brenda."

"Then show it." Her voice rose. "Show it, Michael. Don't rush off
every chance you get to go do some work. That's all you do. Work.
Work. Work. Even though Dr. Martin has warned you to slow
down."

Michael looked at her.

"Yes, I know all about it." She stepped back. "Although you didn't
tell me. I ran into him at the grocery store and we started talking.
The next thing I know he's asking me have you slowed down any.

And he's telling me how he told you you really need to. Then he's talking about your heart and I'm thinking, I didn't know anything about any of this. I know nothing about my own husband." Brenda flung her arms toward the ceiling. "I don't even know that he's having health problems because he didn't tell me. He doesn't share anything with me, except for his big house and our wonderful cars and how great we look to the public."

Michael turned his back and pulled a light green shirt off of another hanger. "I didn't want to concern you, Brenda. I didn't want you to worry."

"Well I am concerned," Brenda replied. "I'm concerned about that. I'm concerned about our marriage. I'm concerned that I may never have a baby. Never."

Michael began to put on the shirt. "And that is what this is really all about, isn't it?" He looked at her. "And it's not just about your not having a baby." His volume dropped. "It's about Cora having one."

"Don't you throw Cora's baby up to me, Michael. Don't you do it." She pointed. "I wanted a baby before Cora and Warren got married. I wanted a baby, but I lost my baby. So don't you show me that in that department too, that I don't measure up to Cora." Brenda trembled.

"It's not me that's doing the comparing, Brenda." Michael's eyes were sad. "It's you."

"You say you're not comparing . . ." She shook her head. "How can I not compare us, Michael? When, ever since Cora married Warren, you have made love to me less and less. And you work like some crazy man. Every day. Day in and day out. Weekends. Nights. It doesn't matter to you."

"I'm sorry you don't like the way I've chosen to make a living for us. When everything I do is for us."

"No it's not," she said quietly. Tears filled her eyes. "You're doing it so you can forget how you feel about my sister. Well, you can work yourself to death, Michael Dawson, and I don't think

you'll ever be able to forget her." Brenda sobbed. "And no matter
what I do, I don't think I'll ever be able to make you forget her. It's
my punishment"—she choked up—"for loving you after all you've
been to my family. To both my sisters. It's my punishment."

"Brenda . . . Don't. Don't." He pulled her into his arms. "Don't
do this." Michael kissed her forehead, then tried to wipe her tears
away. "Don't cry. Why should God punish you? You've tried to do
nothing but good." He gently kissed her. "Look. I'll stay home
tonight. I'll give my client a call and tell him something very important has come up."

Brenda continued to sniffle but her eyes brightened.

"We'll have that quiet evening you want," Michael continued.
"That I want. I want peace of mind just like you." His eyes turned
desperate. "And I'm going to do everything I can to help us have
the life that we deserve."

"I love you." Brenda put her arms around Michael and he kissed
her in a way he hadn't in a long, long time.

Nebia's Story . . .

"I've got to give it to them," Erica said, "they keep trying. They
keep working on that marriage. Whatever little marriage they had."

"I know that's right," Sheila replied. "Shoot. Every time I think
that Michael's going to explode or that Brenda's going to say dee-
vorce." She waved her hand across her face. "This never-give-up
spirit just comes and Michael reaches out to Brenda again. I tell
you, it's the most amazing thing."

"It is," Cynthia replied. "So I guess he did love Brenda. At least
he wanted a home with her. But he loved Cora, too. What a mess."

"Yes, he did," Nebia said. "Michael loved both of them. But he had
made a life with Brenda, and being the kind of man that he was, he
couldn't turn his back on that."

"I-I-I don't know," Cynthia said. "What if Cora was free? What if

Cora hadn't married Warren? How much turning back would he have done?"

Nebia paused. "Well . . . I guess that's something we'll never know, because Cora did marry Warren, and Michael and Brenda continued to try to hold their marriage together."

Chapter 27

"Mommy. I want bubble. I want bubble, Mommy."

"Faith, we agreed to wait until we got home to blow bubbles," Cora said.

"I want bubble now, Mommy." Faith's chubby fingers tried to unscrew the top of the plastic bottle.

"All right. Okay. Just two blows." Cora knelt in front of the door of the Five and Ten. She placed her purse and a small bag on the ground. "Here, let me help you." Cora gazed at Faith's intense face as she took the pink container and unscrewed the top. Carefully, she removed the bubble wand. "Okay, now. Blow." She put it near her daughter's mouth. Unconsciously, Cora pursed her lips, too.

Faith blew several times, but no bubble formed.

"Let me show you," Cora offered. She brought the wand to her mouth and blew slowly. A large bubble bloomed. They both watched as it detached itself and floated into the air.

"Look, Mommy! Look! Bubble. Bubble."

"Ye-es. It's a bubble." Cora laughed and kissed Faith on the cheek.

"It's a bubble." Faith's little finger pointed and followed the rise of the incandescent circle as it floated up and in front of Brenda, who had stopped a few feet away.

"Hi, Cora."

"Brenda. Hello." Cora rose to her feet.

"Mommy." Faith tugged at her dress. "You said two bubbles. Make another one."

Cora picked up her belongings, then situated Faith in her arms. "Okay. One more." She dipped the wand in the bubble mix and blew. Several small bubbles emerged from the quick burst of air.

Faith grinned. Cora smiled then looked at Brenda, whose eyes lingered on Faith's face.

"How are you?" Cora asked.

"I'm fine," Brenda replied. "And you? The two of you?"

"We're good. Say hi, Faith. This is your Aunt Brenda."

Faith looked at Brenda then lay her head against her mother's breast. Finally, she wriggled her fingers.

Cora looked back at Brenda. "We decided to come down here and pick up a few things."

"I've got a little shopping to do myself," Brenda replied.

"Look at you. Aren't you thin?" Cora said. "As thin as those models in some of the magazines." She smiled. "But I guess you look at me and say I've gained weight."

"You look wonderful, Cora. Just as any mother should. You look absolutely wonderful," Brenda repeated.

Cora looked into her sister's disillusioned eyes and looked away. "When we were growing up, did you ever think it would end up this way?" She looked back at Brenda. "I didn't."

"Neither did I." Brenda's grip tightened on her purse. Her face saddened.

"But life could be worse," Cora said.

Brenda nodded. "Sure it could."

Cora nodded too. "I'll tell Mama I saw you."

Brenda placed her purse in front of her. "Thanks."

Their eyes locked.

"Bye." Hesitantly, Brenda touched Cora's cheek, then Faith's hair. "Bye, Faith." Brenda said the toddler's name softly before she entered into the revolving door.

Cora and Faith went straight to Laura's place. She took the Ben-Gay and BC Powder out of the brown bag, and placed them on the kitchen counter. "Mama?" she called.

"I'm back here putting some things away," Laura replied. "I did some washing."

"Come on, Faith. Let's see what your grandmother's up to."

Cora took Faith's hand and followed her mother's voice into Laura's bedroom. "I got the things you asked for. I put them on the counter in the kitchen."

"Thank you, sweetie." Laura smushed the clothes inside the drawer.

Cora leaned against a nearby wall. "Faith and I bumped into Brenda as we were leaving."

Laura continued putting the clothes away.

"She looked like one of those models you see in the magazines," Cora said. "Dressed to kill, she was. And so thin, Mama. Brenda's so thin."

"She said she was doing okay?" Laura didn't look at Cora.

"She said things were fine. I just—don't know if that was really true."

"Well you can't know any more than what she'll tell you." Laura closed the drawer.

Cora sighed. "It's amazing to me that we all live in the same area and we just don't see each other."

"Well we all got our lives, and we go about them the best way we can." Laura cleared her throat. "We're different, that's all. Got different ways of doing things. And I don't think nobody's right and nobody's wrong. So we keep goin', and that's how it's suppose to be." Laura focused on Faith, who had climbed onto her bed and was picking at the nodules of yarn that stuck up from the pale green bedspread.

"Sometimes," Cora began, "but I don't obsess about it, I wish that we could start all over again. That we could all be together the way that I thought we would when I was a girl growing up."

Laura clasped her hands in her lap. "It does no good to try to re-make the past, Cora. No good at all. Don't cause nothing but a bunch of heartache and I've had my share of that. I'm not going to fish for no more." Laura's chin tilted stubbornly. "I'm not going to fish for no more."

Nebia's Story . . .

"Lo-ord," Erica exclaimed. "I don't know if I could take it. I think one of us would have to leave town or something." She looked at the night sky. "How do you do it? Walk around seeing your sister once in a blue moon and when you see her you don't know what to say. Yuck! It's too much for me."

"Yeah I'd say that would be rough," Sheila replied. "But you know, we know folks right now that know their sister or brother, or some relative lives nearby, and they don't have nothing to say to each other because they have had a falling out, a fight or some-thing. So what can you say? When it comes to families, there are all kinds."

"But I'm not talking about those kind of folks. To me it seemed like Cora and Brenda wanted to love each other. They wanted to be sisters again. Didn't they, Nebia?"

"Yes, they did. They surely did. But they just didn't know how to get it going again. So they just kept going. They had things that oc-cupied them and kept their minds away from the heartache. And then of course there was Laura." She licked her lips. "It wasn't just Brenda and Cora; Laura was in it too. You know we older folks can be more stubborn than most. And Laura was as stubborn as they come. So everybody just continued the best way they knew how. That's how life is." Nebia leaned forward. "You just keep going until something stops you in your tracks."

Chapter 28

The main door of The Way Home opened again. Cora glanced up as four young men with black stocking masks slipped inside. Systematically, two of them pulled down the shades so no one could see inside.

"What's going on?" Cora asked as her eyes darted from man to man.

Once the shades were drawn, the men moved slowly, very slowly, as if they were in a play. Three of the intruders went around the room touching things before they became destructive. They knocked over a can of paint, broke chalk, and tore up some of the charcoal etchings.

"Why are you doing this?" Cora demanded. "What is this about? I don't have but a little bit of money in here. If you want the money, I'll give it to you." Cora opened a nearby drawer, but the vandalism continued.

Many of the children's paintings were destroyed. Finally Cora couldn't take it anymore. "Damn it! Say something! If you're going to rob me, rob me! Whatever you've got in mind, do it, and get out of here. Or tell me what this is about."

"You are something else." The only intruder who had stood by and watched spoke. "Here there is four of us, and you've got the nerve to tell us we better speak up." He rose from where he had perched on top of an old armchair. "I'll tell you what this is about, since you just have to know. This is about your cutting into the numbers."

"Cutting into the numbers?" Cora looked at the other vandalizers who were moving toward her.

"Our numbers. The Gangster Disciples." The spokesman hit his chest. "You know, you've been a one-woman show over here and you've got a lot of attention. I'll give you props for that." He removed his skull cap, and the knotted end of his stocking cap mask bobbed. "You've impressed us all, and you've definitely impressed some of the young men that we intended to join us. But now, because of you, and this"—he looked around—"they've decided that they don't want to. And not only don't they want to join us, they've gotten bold enough to tell us what they're not going to do." He shook his head. "We can't have that."

Cora looked defiant. "Well maybe you need to change what you do. I can't help it if what I offer appeals to them. Maybe my way feels better. Maybe it's safer. You need to think about that." Her eyes blazed. "Here the four of you come in here like this against one defenseless woman. You can't feel good about that. And if you do, I can't imagine why. So I think while you've got a chance, you better take this money"—she laid thirty-some-odd dollars out on the table—"and leave now. If you do, you won't hear a peep from me." She crossed her arms. "And maybe your conscience will hound you bad enough that you won't ever try something like this again."

One of the young men laughed. "I can't believe it. She's threatening us. She is one bold bitch. Telling us to leave and hopefully our conscience is going to get us." He laughed again, then stopped abruptly. "Lady, I don't have no conscience." He grabbed another painting and ripped it down the middle. "This is what I think about you and my conscience." He grabbed another one.

Cora was across the room before she knew it. "You stop that.

Don't you do that!" She grabbed the painting and the young man caught her arm. Cora looked at his wrist tattooed with an open-mouthed snake devouring the world.

"What's wrong with you? Are you crazy? I'll break your arm."

"No, I'm not crazy. You must be crazy. All of you. You get out of here. You hear me? You get out of here right now before you do something you regret."

Suddenly, the door to The Way Home swung open and Cora looked at the clock. It was nine P.M., the time Warren dropped by every evening to check on her.

"Cora, why are the shades drawn?" Warren asked as he stepped inside.

"Warren," Cora shouted.

"Let's get out of here," one intruder shouted.

A mad dash toward Warren and the door ensued.

"Stop where you are," Warren commanded, and reached for his gun, but before he could draw, the Gangster Disciples grabbed him.

"What the fuck we gon' do now?" another one said. "If we leave him we're going to jail."

"Hold off, man," the spokesman demanded as Warren and two of the gang members struggled.

"Just go," Cora pleaded. "Go! He won't arrest you. Tell them, Warren. You're not going to arrest them. You're not going to do anything."

"What were you doing in here?" Warren demanded as he tried to free himself. "You're not going to get away with this."

"Shut up! Shut up! Shit," one of the young men exploded. "See, I wasn't down for none of this. All this here . . . You know we were suppose to be just scaring her, but now what the fuck we gon' do? Look at this shit."

"I'll show you what I'm going to do," the most violent gang member declared. He drew back then thrust forward. Warren cried out in pain.

"Fuck! Let's get out of here," the spokesman yelled as Warren slumped to the floor.

"Warren!" Cora ran to him as the young men headed out the door. She fell to her knees. "Warren! Oh my God! He stabbed you! Warren!"

Warren groaned and grabbed near his heart.

"Warren. Hold on, baby. I'm going to call for help."

Cora ran to the telephone and dialed the operator. "Please call an ambulance. This is Cora Gray. My husband, Warren Gray, a policeman, has been stabbed. So please come to 1526 4th Street South. Please! Hurry!"

"You say your husband has been stabbed?"

"Yes! He's a policeman and he's hurt bad. Please send an ambulance to 1526 4th Street South."

The operator repeated the address. "I'll send an ambulance right away."

"Hurry!" Cora shouted before she hung up and returned to Warren's side. He groaned again when she touched his arm. "You're going to be all right now. An ambulance is on its way." She stroked his face. "Just lie still. Lie still." Cora tried to calm Warren and herself, but her breath staggered when she saw how the blood seemed to pour from his body.

Cora ran for one of the towels she kept in the back room. When she returned she knelt down by Warren's side and unbuttoned the top of his uniform. There was a gaping wound that looked as if it had been made by a jagged object. "Oh baby." Cora's tears ran as she placed the towel over the bloody hole. Then she covered it with his uniform. "You're going to be all right, Warren. You are." She looked at his face.

"Cora." Warren could barely say her name. "Everything's going dark, Cora."

"No. No, it's not dark," she commanded. "It's still light in here." She pointed to the bare lightbulb above them.

Weakly, Warren shook his head from side to side. "I feel it's getting darker. I feel myself slipping away, Cora. I do."

"No, Warren. Don't say that. You're not slipping away. You're not."

"Cora, listen to me." He tugged at her sleeve. "Listen to me, baby." Warren tried to focus on her face. "I feel myself slipping away. I feel myself dying."

"Oh God! Warren. No-o!" she cried. "No Warren! No! You can't die! Warren, please! I can't take it if you die. I can't. Please, Warren. I can't take it."

"I'm sorry. I'm sorry to leave you, Cora. All I can tell you is, I love you. I loved you from the moment I saw you as a boy, and now I've loved you until the day I died. Take care of Faith." He swallowed. "I know you will pour on her all the love you would have given the two of us."

"No," Cora cried softly. "No."

But even as she cried, Warren's hand slipped from her sleeve and dropped to the floor.

"This cannot be." Cora looked at his closed eyes. "Warren! Warren!" She lifted his head onto her lap and laid her face against his. "Warren. My lover. My friend. How can I let you go? How? How?"

Nebia's Story . . .

"And they say that's how they found them. Warren was dead with his head in her lap and Cora was asking how."

"No way, Miss Nebia. Don't tell me that." Erica wiped away tears before she began to pace the porch. "This just can't be happening."

"So Warren died," Sheila said. "This is horrible. God! Life can be just horrible. So Cora lost her baby sister, then she lost her husband."

"Yes, she did." Nebia shook her head.

"Were the guys who did it arrested?" Cynthia asked.

"Who were they going to arrest?" Nebia asked. "The young men wore stockings over their faces, and Cora didn't tell the authorities anything."

"But you said Cora saw one of the men had a tattoo," Sheila said. "They could have identified him from that."

"Of course they could," Nebia replied. "Cora knew that. But Cora being Cora, she had her own plan. With Warren dying like that, it triggered something in her that was pure destruction itself."

Chapter 29

"Come on here, baby. Come sit on grandma's lap while Nebia rolls us up to the stairs." Laura looked at Lucille, who waited on the porch. She had aged ten years.

Faith went into Laura's arms, and with one big heave Laura pulled her onto her lap. "We're going inside the house and have a little bit to eat. You hungry?"

"I'm hungry," Faith replied.

"Good. Grandma will fix you a nice plate."

"Yes, ma'am." Faith leaned over the arm of the wheelchair and looked back at her mother. "Grandma?"

"Yes, baby."

"Why is Mommy crying?"

"Aw-w, mama's sad, little one. She's just real sad."

"I've never seen Mommy cry so much before."

"Hush now, Faith. Just hush, and let her have her moment. Okay?"

"Where's Daddy? Mommy said we left him back there at that place, but I didn't see him."

"We did leave him back there, sugar. We had to. Like we told you, your daddy's gone now. He's with . . ." Laura paused. "God."

"With God?" Faith's small brow wrinkled. "Have I ever met Him?"

"Well . . . in a way you have, because He's always with us."

"But I don't remember seeing Him, Grandma."

"I'll make it clear one day, but right now you just hush." They reached the stairs. "Now let me put you down. You know Grandma and Grandma Nebia got to make a production out of my getting out of this chair and going up these stairs."

Faith followed while Nebia served as a counterweight for Laura as she took one stair at a time. Laura reached the top and turned around to give Faith a hand.

"What do you want?" Cora yelled and Faith began to cry.

"What?" She challenged a group of young men who had gathered in front of the house next door.

"We're not doing nothin' to you," one of them replied with a hard face. "We're just standing here lookin'."

"What you looking at? Tell me, what do you see?" Cora took a couple of steps toward them.

"Cora now, wait a minute," Laura warned.

"Tell me. What do you see?" Cora continued. "Are you standing here because you want to comfort me? Are you standing here because you're sorry that my husband's dead?"

"Look, we ain't said nothin' to you," another man said.

"No, you haven't said anything to me. Not one thing. And why is that? You can stand here in a group and just watch my misery but you don't say nothing." More tears flowed. "Even now, you could have said 'I'm sorry, Mrs. Gray, that your husband's gone.' But you didn't. Could that be because you know who killed him?"

One of boys threw up his hands. "I don't know nothing about nothing."

"You don't, do you? You don't know nothing about nothing. And that's a shame. But I want you to know this, Warren Gray was a good man. He could have been either one of your fathers, or your uncle, because he would have looked after you. He would have tried to tell you right because he tried to live right." She pounded her fist into her palm. "Do you understand that? Do you understand a person who has tried to live their life right, doing good by others? And what it means to those that love them when they're just snuffed out in some kind of crazy incident that should never have happened?"

Some of the men looked down. Others looked at each other.

"No. You don't understand," Cora continued. "And you'll never understand my pain. But I tell you this, I'm putting a warning out to any and all members of the Gangster Disciples, that this black woman, this black woman is going to avenge her husband's death. I am not going to allow him to die without those who are responsible feeling some of our pain."

One of the young men's shoulders rose up and down. "So, what you saying, man?" He stepped forward as if he were about to fight. "Are you threatening us?"

"Do I look like I'm threatening you?" She squinted and fire shot from her eyes. "Do I look like it? If you feel me now, I want you to know every ancestor I've ever known, every ancestor of your ancestors, of The Ancestors." Her arms shot out in front of her and her fingers splayed. "I call on them now, and I mean what I say, that I will see those that are responsible for the death of my husband feeling his pain."

The young man stood stark still.

"She crazy, man," one of the others said.

"She's as crazy as they come. She done been to Africa and think she can put some of that black magic stuff on you." They started laughing and making funny faces.

"Laugh," Cora said. "You laugh now, but I want to see who's going to be laughing last. 'Cause I'm going to call down every soul that might help me. Every way I've ever heard of that might take care of whoever was responsible." She pointed at each one of them.

Nebia placed her hand on Cora's arm and she turned and looked at her. "Come on, now. Come on in here and settle down before all the folks start arriving." She pulled a reluctant Cora toward her.

When Cora got to the top of the stairs she picked up Faith. She was sobbing. "Don't cry, my sweetness." Cora held her close. "Mommy didn't mean to frighten you."

"Why were you hollering, Mommy?"

"I've got my reasons, sugar. I've got my reasons." She turned back and looked at the young men, who had moved up the street a bit.

When Cora entered her mother's house, all the strength that anger had given her ebbed away, and she collapsed into a chair with Faith on her lap.

Nebia's Story . . .

"Boy! Cora flipped out there for a minute, didn't she?" Sheila said.

"Cora was thinking about her husband being dead," Cynthia replied. "And here these young things are, standing there watching. I don't blame her. What were they watching for?"

"Well she might have thought all that stuff, but I don't know how wise it was to say it," Sheila said. "Shoot, here Laura, Lucille and you"—she looked at Nebia—"are living by yourselves, and now Cora too. . . . You have to be careful."

"I know that's right," Cynthia replied.

Finally Nebia said, "Cora didn't care. She was so hurt when she lost Warren she just didn't care. And Cora wanted to strike back. She wanted them to know, she wanted to get at them. So what did she do? She tried to put fear in their hearts the only way she knew how. A way that Cora hoped would gnaw at them when they were alone. She wasn't about guns and knives, but knew about other worldly things. Cora knew about herbs and calling in the spirits. She'd seen it done in Africa. So Cora threatened them with what she knew had put fear in the hearts of others."

"Them young hoods weren't scared of no ghosts. The ones I know aren't. Boy, they'd try to shoot a ghost if they saw one."

All three of them snickered.

"Yeah, well," Nebia remarked, "I understand what you're saying, but I bet if you could be a fly on the wall when one of them young men was lying in his bed and he started hearing strange noises, and maybe he feels something move across his face—say a cold hand that he can't see—you'd see how brave, and how much shootin' would help him then."

"Invisible, cold hands on your face," Cynthia said. "Now that's a whole different subject. I think anybody would be scared."

"And that's what Cora believed."

"Did she really do anything like that?" Erica asked.

"No." Nebia shook her head. "Cora bided her time, that's what she did. And her desire for revenge increased. Because you've got to understand, Cora was crazy with grief. Crazy. Crazed because she was grieving again at such a young age for somebody she loved."

Chapter 30

"Afternoon, Laura. Nebia."

Nebia nodded and Laura replied, "Hello Bertha. How you doing?"

"I'm fine."

"So what you got there?" Laura asked. "I thought it was just old folks like me"—she held up her prescription bag—"that had to come up here to the pharmacist to get medicine all the time."

Bertha laughed. "I guess old man time catches up with all of us. I got a couple of prescriptions here. I tell you my blood pressure just won't do nothing but go sky high. I'm tryin' to do whatever they tell me but it's been such a trial. So they upped the dosage, and we're hopin' it'll do me some good."

"I know the feeling," Laura replied.

"How about you?" Bertha looked at Nebia. "You on any medications?"

"I'm on my herbs. Anything come up with me, my herbs can take care of it. I've never taken a prescription medication in my life, and I don't intend to."

"Well aren't you one lucky soul," Bertha replied.

Laura leaned in. "Or nutty one."

The two women laughed. Nebia rolled her eyes.

"Is your grandson still going to The Way Home?" Laura inquired.

Bertha looked uneasy. "No-o. The truth is, I don't think he's been for a couple of weeks now."

"Really. Is he sick?" Laura pressed.

"No. No, his mama said she just don't want him to go anymore."

"She doesn't?" Laura's brow folded.

"No-o."

"Why is that, Bertha? It seems like Cora's been having quite a few of the kids dropping out lately. She said something about it to me the other day."

"I can imagine." Bertha nodded. "This world is one crazy place, isn't it? And you know when it's like that, you've got to be careful. And that's how my daughter sees it. She's afraid because some of them gang members are secretly threatening folks. They say if you let your child go to Cora's then you might have trouble somewhere else. So my daughter decided it just wasn't worth it. And that's the truth."

"Say what?" Laura sat forward in her wheelchair.

"You didn't know nothing about it?"

"No, this is the first time I've heard anything like that. You, Nebia?"

"Not a word."

"Yeah, chile. This has been one crazy mess, because you know folks like Cora and everythin', especially the children, but people are afraid. You don't know what these young boys gon' do. So when they start spreading the word that you might not like what happens if you continue to send your child up there, it's an easy decision to make."

Laura folded her hands and looked down. "I guess it would be."

"And you need to be concerned for your daughter too, Laura. I know she's lost her husband and ain't nothin' sadder than that, outside of losin' her sister." Bertha swallowed. "But I can only think if they're threatening us . . . what might happen to her." She looked away. "I just—I don't even want to think about it."

Laura looked at Nebia. "I tell you, if it's not one thing it's another."

"Well, I hate to be the one to tell you, Laura, but since you didn't know, I had to tell you the truth."

"Sure you did, Bertha. I appreciate it."

"Well, maybe you should warn Cora. These boys are serious. They ain't playin' no game. You know the kind of stuff that's been goin' on around here. A house burned down the other day up the street. And they don't know what happened there."

"What about the neighborhood watch program? Isn't it doing any good?" Laura shook her head.

"Yes, some. You get to know what's happening and who has had some problems. Of course everybody's lookin' out for each other. But I tell you, it's wild. Even with all we're doin' to try to stay on top of it, the bad element seems to be able to get in here, do their dirt. Not only are they burning down houses, but there are many more drugs being sold, too. I just don't know how they doin' it. And the drugs aren't doin' nothin' but makin' these young folks even crazier. I speak to you from my heart now, Laura." Bertha wiped her nose. "That's why I liked it when my grandson was going to The Way Home. He had a different attitude about things. He seemed to be hopeful. But now that Cicely has stopped him from going, he seems to have sunken into this dark hole, and some of them old boys we didn't like to see him with started hangin' around again. But what are we to do?"

"Yes." Laura sighed. "What are we to do?"

"Well I tell you, it's a shame that you can't have the kind of business that you want just because other folks got plans that aren't nearly as high-minded as yours. It's just a shame." Bertha sighed. "And I'm sorry that Cora's got to deal with this. But she's goin' to have to. I'm really afraid for her and for this neighborhood." She bit her lip. "And from the word that's going around, I don't think

she's going to have many kids going there. I think you might pre-
pare her for that, because the time is comin', and she needs to get
her ducks in a row."

"All right, Bertha," Laura replied.

"Well, you take care now," Bertha said. "Both of you."

"You do the same," Nebia said, and they watched her walk away.

"What's next?" Laura said under her breath. "They have taken
her husband away, and now they about to put her out of business.
Why in the world can't that child find no peace? Hasn't she dealt
with enough?" She slammed her prescription bag down in her lap.
"And that old church and Community Ties and all that mess, why
can't they do something? They got pull in our neighborhood.
You'd think they'd gather everybody together and say support her.
She's doing good."

In a low voice Nebia replied, "You know they're not going to do
that. Cora's been on the wrong side of the fence ever since she
opened that place. Had she been more like them, they would help
her now."

Nebia's Story . . .

"Did you end up telling Cora what that woman said?" Cynthia
asked.

"We told her. As a matter of fact, Laura told her later that evening."

"Oh my goodness. I guess she was hurt even more," Erica replied.

"No. No, she wasn't," Nebia said.

"She wasn't?" Sheila said with disbelief.

"No. When Laura told Cora what Bertha said, Cora just kind of
sat back and got this real strange smile on her face. For a minute I
thought she had totally lost it. I just couldn't understand, and the
next thing I knew she was saying how she understood. That she
didn't want to be bringing bad to the neighborhood and having
folks afraid for their children, and for themselves. Cora said she
was going to bring an end to it all. She said she was going to close

The Way Home down. She set a date right there. Said that every-body would be invited including the Gangster Disciples and there would be food and everything. Cora said she would make a peace offering with the closing."

"How long was this after Warren's funeral?" Sheila asked.

"No more than two months."

"And in that amount of time Cora had decided to let it go?" Cynthia crossed her arms.

"I don't believe it." Erica jumped in. "I thought you said revenge had built up in her."

"It had. But with a mind like Cora's you could never guess what she was going to do. That's what she told us at the time, and we were just as shocked as you are now. But see, only Cora knew what she had planned."

Chapter 31

"Would you care for some more chicken?" Cora said to an elderly man with an empty plate.

"Is there enough for me to have a little more?" he asked.

"Of course." Cora steadied the Styrofoam plate that shook in his hand, and gave him another drumstick.

Cora looked at the door, then around the room. The Way Home was packed. People had come and gone all afternoon. Again her anxious gaze strayed to the door.

"Hello." A man stuck his hand out. "I'm Reverend Benson. How you doing this evening?"

"I'm fine, reverend. How are you?" Cora replied.

"Good. I'd like to take this opportunity and invite you to my church. All Faith Church. You've probably heard of it."

"I have," Cora replied.

"Maybe we'll see you at service one day."

"Maybe."

Reverend Benson cleared his throat. "You've got some really good food here, too."

"Thank you," Cora said. "I cooked everything myself."

"You're quite the cook," Reverend Benson replied.

"Thank you," Cora said again and looked at the door.

"I have to say I'm sad that you've decided to close this place down."

Cora looked directly into his eyes. "Are you really?"

"Yes, I am," he said, holding on to the lie. "But-uh, it's hard to keep things going in this neighborhood unless you have a support system. So the next time you decide to open up a business, why don't you come and talk to us at the church; we're always willing to get behind good causes. And as you probably know, your sister, Brenda, is very involved in Community Ties. She and her husband, Michael, are members of our congregation."

"I'm aware of that." Cora continued to look deep in his eyes until the reverend looked away.

"Well, I hope you keep what I said in mind."

"You can believe I won't forget it," Cora replied, before he walked away.

"Now what was so scary about this place?" Cora overheard the question. "I don't see nothing in here that would frighten me."

"You wouldn't right now. I hear she cleared some things out of here this morning. But there was all kinds of stuff up in here. That's why I came here today, just to see."

"Well, I don't believe it. I didn't believe it when I heard it before, and I don't believe it now. So here you are eating her food and everything, just to be nosey."

Cora turned to see who was talking, but the door opened again. Two more young men came in. There was something familiar about one of them. They spoke to several people in the room, including Reverend Benson. Once or twice they gazed in her direction but kept their distance.

Cora walked over to them. "Hello."

"What's happenin'?" the taller one said. The other said nothing.

"Welcome to The Way Home." Cora smiled. "I don't think I've ever seen you around here before."

"You haven't."

The second voice held a familiar tone and Cora's hands began to shake. She put them behind her. "Still, I'm glad to meet so many people even though The Way Home is closing. Can I offer you something to eat?"

"I could eat," the first man said. "We heard you was really doin' it over here. That's why we came out."

"Well, whenever you're ready, come over to the table"—she pointed—"and I'll fix your plates."

"We could do that right now," the quietest one replied.

"Fine. Let's start with some punch." Cora led the way. She ladled up a mixture of cherry Kool-Aid and pineapple juice and handed the quietest man a cup. He reached out and Cora caught a glimpse of a snake swallowing the world on his wrist. Her body trembled but she continued to smile. "Now let me get you something to eat. Oh-h"—Cora looked at the table—"I need to freshen up that potato salad." She picked up the dish. "You wait here. I'll go get a fresh batch."

Cora went into the back room. She stopped in front of the counter and held on to it. "That's him," she said softly. "That's the Gangster Disciple that killed Warren." Cora continued to lean against the counter before she forced herself to stand. "I can't be weak now. Not now."

Quickly, Cora reached in the back of the refrigerator and pulled out a bowl of potato salad. She put some on both plates. She pushed the remains of the dish deep into the back of a cabinet. Cora dipped fresh potato salad from another container into the large rectangular tin before she carried it back out front.

"Okay. Here we are." She smiled again. Cora placed fried chicken, bread, baked beans, and a small ear of corn on their plates. She handed the food to the gangsters.

"Thank you," the tallest one said. The one with the tattoo simply nodded before they went and stood in the corner and ate by themselves. No sooner had they finished eating, they left.

A couple of hours later when all the people had gone home, Cora locked the doors to The Way Home for the last time. Nebia helped her carry the few items that remained to her car.

"Things turned out well," Nebia said.

"Perfect," Cora replied. Her jaw was hard. "I couldn't have planned it any better."

Nebia looked at her.

Cora pushed the containers she carried onto the car seat. "I bet Faith has worn Mama out by now," she remarked.

"No doubt," Nebia replied.

"Since we moved back home they've been as thick as thieves." Cora smiled a sad smile. "I'm glad they got to come by a little earlier and eat a little something. I wanted Mama to be a part of this."

"Well, she was," Nebia said. "But I noticed Brenda didn't make it."

"No, but Michael called. He said Brenda wasn't feeling well. That she's got a doctor's appointment tomorrow."

Nebia nodded as they put more things on the backseat. Finally, Nebia climbed into the front, but Cora remained standing outside. She stared at The Way Home. "I'll never forget this place, Nebia."

"How can you?" Nebia looked through the open window at the old building.

Early the next morning Nebia went for a walk. She greeted all the familiar faces along the way. Things had gone well until she bumped into a gossipy neighbor.

"Morning, Nebia. I see you out early this morning," Mary said.

"Aren't I always?" Nebia replied.

Mary didn't answer. "Guess what I heard?"

"What have you heard this time?" Nebia continued on her way.

Mary fell in step with her. "There was a boy that died early this morning."

"What boy?" Nebia asked.

"One of those Gangster Disciples. They say he got real sick, him and a friend of his, with some kind of stomach trouble. Possibly food poisoning. One of them turned out all right, but the other one had what the doctors called some complications, and he died."

Nebia's expression and pace never changed. "Did they say where they got the food poisoning?"

"The folks downtown traced all the places they'd been. They'd been to one of those hamburger joints, but they also went to Cora's thing at The Way Home."

Nebia continued in silence before she said, "Give my condolences to the family. I know you know them. You know everybody."

Mary looked self-important. "Of course I know them. And I'll tell them what you said."

Mary went on her way and Nebia walked on down the street. When she got back to the house, she went straight into the Robinsons' place. Cora was in the kitchen cooking breakfast. Laura was sitting in her wheelchair at the kitchen table with a cup of coffee. Faith was playing with a worn-out teddy bear.

"Morning, Nebia," Cora greeted her. "You want some breakfast?"

"I'm not hungry," Nebia said. "Not this morning."

"You always eat a little something." Cora stirred the grits. "What's wrong?"

Nebia sat down. "While I was on my walk, I heard a young man died last night."

"Who?" Cora looked at her.

"One of those Gangster Disciples. Seem like he and a buddy of his got food poisoning." Nebia looked at Faith. "Both of them got real sick, but the one that died had some complications."

"I see." Cora focused on the steaming cereal. She stirred them again.

"They say the authorities are trying to figure out where they got it from," Nebia continued. "One of the places they went yesterday was to The Way Home, Cora."

"Really?" Cora replied.

"Cora." Laura spoke for the first time. "You don't know nothing about this, do you?"

Cora stopped stirring. "I don't know nothing about nobody dying," she replied, then added softly, "Maybe a higher power did what I couldn't bring myself to do."

"Cora." Laura gasped.

Faith looked at her grandmother and then her mother.

"I didn't intend for nobody to leave here, Mama." Cora went and stood by her wheelchair. "If I had they would both be in the morgue today. Yes, I had revenge in my heart. I wanted them to suffer. I wanted them to think they were going to die, but no . . . I couldn't just take a human life."

Nebia's Story . . .

"Cora poisoned them," Cynthia said, shocked.

Nebia looked at the moon. "Cora used some herbs that she knew would make them sick. Awful sick. But Cora had no way of knowing there would be complications and one of them would end up dead."

"Oh my God!" Erica exclaimed. "That's still like . . . murder. He died from the herbs she put in that potato salad."

"Ends up he died from kidney failure," Nebia replied. "He had taken some drugs, too." Nebia looked at each one of them. "So who was to say?"

"But the police had to come and question Cora? Did they arrest her?" Sheila pressed.

Nebia closed her eyes. "Things happened so fast, it never got to that."

Chapter 32

"What you need to do is remain calm," said Reverend Benson. "Not keeping your head at a time like this will surely cause trouble."

"Reverend, we're done listening to you, old man. We simply came here to tell you this good-guy role that you wanted us to play ain't gon' cut it." The young man stood up. "We've been coming around here playing the game the way you wanted it just because you were keeping a little money in our pockets. You said as long as we kept the violence down, you'd keep us employed. Well thank you for doing your part, but it's all over now. That woman killed Thomas and now we gon' take care of her. That's just the way it goes." He squinted. "Don't the Bible say an eye for an eye and a tooth for a tooth?"

Reverend Benson stood as well. "Please! You can't be serious. You're upset and you don't know what you're saying."

"Sit down," the Disciple said. "I know what I'm saying. You're the one that don't understand. You the one that's the big hypocrite." He pointed in the Reverend's face. "Now that this woman has killed Thomas you want us to ignore the part of the Bible that says an eye for an eye and a tooth for a tooth. How is it, Reverend, that you pick and choose what you want to use out of that Bible?" His lip curled. "Naw-aw. I see how you want to play this. You just use that book any way that suits you so you can keep riding in your Cadillac and living in your big fancy house. 'Cause now when I tell you that we're going to take that bitch, Cora Gray, out, you want to stop us. So what's right and what's wrong, Reverend? Where do you draw your line when it comes to sin?"

"Don't do this to yourselves," Reverend Benson reasoned.

"It's a little late for you to say that. Because by tomorrow morning, she gon' be gone." The gangster walked backwards. "And if you tell anybody that I said so, your next sermon might be a silent one, from a casket." He opened the door. "Let's go," he said to his companion.

Michael's heart jumped when he heard the threat against Cora, followed by footsteps headed toward the pastor's office door. Quickly, he hurried across the hall into the men's room and into one of the stalls. Michael waited several minutes before he rushed and opened the bathroom door. He nearly bumped into Reverend Benson.

"Reverend," Michael said. They both looked startled.

Michael hurried on. "I was just going to knock on your door and let you know that I've got to cancel our appointment." He looked at his watch. "Can we schedule another time to talk about that investment? I feel it can really help the church in the long run."

Reverend Benson ran a hand over his sweaty forehead. "Sure, we can reschedule."

"I'm in a hurry now." Michael looked at his watch again. "But I'll call you tomorrow and we'll set a time."

Reverend Benson nodded before he wiped his forehead again. He looked up the hall. "I'll talk to you tomorrow."

"Good afternoon," Michael said as he walked to the stairs. Once out of earshot he ran outside to his car and jumped inside. "They're going to kill Cora. They're going to kill her," he said as he started the car. "I can't let that happen. I've got to warn her."

Michael took off for the Robinsons' building. Minutes later he pulled up out front and ran up the walkway and up the stairs. He rang the doorbell several times. Cora answered the door.

"Michael." She looked surprised. "Come in. I haven't seen you since Warren's funeral."

"I've got to talk to you, Cora." He looked around the living room.

"All right," she said.

He went to the window and looked out.

"Who is it?" Laura's voice drifted from the rear of the house.

"It's Michael, Mama."

Michael came back to the center of the room.

"What is it, Michael?" Cora asked as she watched him.

"Did you hear about that young man that died this morning? It involved food poisoning."

Cora looked him straight in the eye. "Yes. Nebia told us about it not too long ago."

Michael didn't seem to be able to catch his breath. "Well his friends think that you are responsible." He shook his head. "They intend to do something about it."

"Like what?" Cora folded her arms.

"God knows what, Cora! What difference does that make?" Michael leaned against the wall. "They intend to do something about it. They intend to get you because they believe you're behind it." He held his head in his hands. "You threatened them. Two of them got sick after being at your place and now one of them is dead."

Cora sat on the couch. She rubbed her hand down her thigh. "Well . . . we shall see."

"No. This is not a we shall see." Michael sat beside her. "This is what are you going to do?" He looked into her eyes. "If they get a chance they are going to kill you."

"They're not going to get a chance. I'll just go to the police and tell them I did not intend for anyone to die." She looked down, then up again. "And that's the truth."

Michael looked away. "You go to the police and tell them you didn't poison them. What difference is that going to make to the Gangster Disciples?" He looked back at her. "You don't understand. I told you they believe you killed him. And they intend to kill you. I heard them say it."

"What?" Laura exclaimed. She rolled her wheelchair forward. Cora looked at her mother, then down at Faith.

"Faith, baby. Go upstairs and look at that book Mommy bought for you. I'll call you and tell you when we're through down here."

Faith looked frightened. "I don't want to—"

"Faith. Please, baby. Go upstairs and read your book. I'll come up when we're done."

"Okay," she said slowly, and ascended the stairs.

Laura waited until Faith was out of sight. "Now what did I hear you say?"

"I heard a couple of those gang members tell Reverend Benson they plan to get revenge for the death of that Gangster Disciple that died this morning."

"Reverend Benson?" Laura said. "What's he got to do with this?"

Michael squeezed his forehead. "It seems he promised some of the gang members honest work as long as they toed the line, but with that boy's death this morning they told Pastor Benson that deal was off."

Laura's eyes filled with apprehension as she looked at Cora.

Michael shook his head. "I've seen different gang members coming in and out of the church before. Reverend Benson's been counseling them, trying to help them change."

"And you say some of those gang members are planning to kill Cora?" Nebia asked.

"I heard it with my own ears," Michael said. "I went to talk to the reverend, and I was coming up the hall when I heard loud voices. So I stopped and listened. That's when I heard it. I heard them say she's going to be gone by tomorrow morning."

"This can't be happening." Laura's face sank with worry.

"But it is," Michael said. "And that's why I'm here." He looked at

Cora. "You've got to leave, Cora. You've got to take your child and go."

Cora sat back. "I'm not going anywhere. St. Petersburg is my home. I was born here and I've finally accepted this is where I belong. I'm not leaving." She pointed downward. "This is the place I'm going to die."

"You're right." Michael almost looked ashen. "If you don't go, you're going to die . . . right here. And it could be before tomorrow morning."

Cora shook her head. "Warren was a policeman. They loved him down there. They wouldn't let anything happen to me."

Michael took hold of Cora's shoulders. "These gang members don't work inside the law. What are you going to do? Go down to the police station and have them lock you up to protect you? Because that's what you'd have to do. But even if you did that, how long would you stay there? Those folks have long memories, Cora. If they don't get you now they'd do it later." Michael let go. "But guess what? If they can't get you during a time that satisfies them, they'd go after your mother. Or Miss Nebia. Or your child."

Cora's eyes grew big. "They wouldn't do that."

Michael simply stared at Cora. The room went silent.

"They'd do anything," Michael finally replied.

"You got to get out of here, Cora." Laura rolled forward. "You've got to leave, baby."

"Leave and go where?" Cora turned to her. "Where am I going to go?"

"I don't know." Tears rolled down Laura's face. "But you got to get out of here. I can't take another one of my children dying before me. I can't." She could barely speak. "You've got to go."

"Oh, no. What have I done?" Cora clutched at her heart.

"You did what you thought you had to do," Laura said.

Nebia nodded.

"And this ain't no time to stop," Laura continued. "You got to get you and that baby out of here."

"But what about you? Michael, you said if they can't get me, they might get Mama or Nebia."

"Your mama and me can take care of ourselves," Nebia said. "We been around on this earth long enough that if something happens to us, maybe it will just be our time. Our due. Don't you worry about us. You worry about you and that child."

Cora closed her eyes. "I don't have anywhere to go."

"Yes you do," Nebia refuted. "You can go back to Africa."

"Africa." Cora looked at her mother.

"You've lived there before." Laura lifted her chin. "And you can live there again. It won't be forever."

"Even if I decided to go back," Cora said, " I don't have money for Faith and I just to jump up and go."

"I've got the money," Michael said. "I'll help you." His love was plain to see. Michael looked down. "I'm sure Brenda and I both will help."

"Michael, I can't ask you to—"

"Don't." He closed his eyes. "Let me do this one thing for you, Cora. Before you go. Please."

Tears rolled down Cora's face. She touched Michael's arm. "All right. I'll take the money."

Michael exhaled.

"But we won't be gone long." Cora looked at Laura. "Just long enough for things to cool down."

"Yes," Laura repeated. "Time heals all kinds of things." But her tears started up again.

Michael stood up. "You get on the phone and make all the arrangements. I'll go right now and get the money from the bank."

Cora stood, too. "I don't know how I'll ever thank you."

"There's no need for thanks between us. You"—his eyes filled with love—"have always been dear to me. All of you," he added quickly. Then he went to the door and opened it. Michael looked at Cora again. "I'll be back within the hour."

* * *

Across town, Brenda walked out of the doctor's office and up to the receptionist's desk.

"So I guess we'll be seeing more of you now." The receptionist smiled.

Brenda smiled, too. "You sure will. She handed the woman a twenty-dollar bill, took her receipt, and walked to the office door. It opened and Brenda stepped aside.

"Hello, Mrs. Dawson."

"Hello, Mrs. Smith. How are you?"

"Doin' just fine. I hope you're well. You look good."

"Thank you." Brenda's smile broadened.

"What a coincidence. I just saw your husband a little while ago."

"You did?"

"Yes. He was going up to your mother's house. It's been such a long time since I've seen y'all over there, so I spoke to him. He waved but he seemed like he was in such a hurry, I didn't say anything else."

"Oh." Brenda's smile vanished.

Mrs. Smith pushed her pocketbook up on her arm. "So it's good seeing you, too."

"Same here," Brenda said and went outside.

She drove up the street. "What was Michael doing over there?" Nervously, she licked her lips. "What could he have been doing?" Brenda stopped at a traffic light. "Now that Warren's dead, has Michael finally decided he wants to be with Cora?" She shook her head. "And here I am going to have a baby."

She started to cross the street when a siren sounded. Brenda could see the ambulance through her rearview mirror. She pulled over to the side and waited. The ambulance passed and Brenda proceeded toward her house. Then she made a sudden turn in the opposite direction. Minutes later Brenda parked out front of her childhood home. She got out, slammed the car door, walked up to the house and rang the doorbell.

Someone peeped through the lace curtains of the front window before the door opened. There Cora stood with tear stains on her face.

"Is Michael here?" Brenda asked.

"Oh, Brenda." Fresh tears flowed. "You don't know," she said softly.

Brenda stared at her. "Know what?"

Cora opened the door farther so Brenda could come inside. Brenda looked at her mother, sitting in her wheelchair, and at Nebia, who stood beside it.

"Michael left here about thirty minutes ago. He got in his car and drove up the street." Cora kept her eyes focused on Brenda's face. "He had a major heart attack, Brenda. The ambulance workers tried to revive him, but they couldn't."

"What?" Brenda looked from one face to another. "Michael is dead?"

Cora covered her face with her hand.

"When the ambulance pulled off they hadn't been able to revive him," Laura said. "There's a strong possibility that he is."

"I just called your house." Cora wiped her eyes.

"Michael was here seeing you, then he had a heart attack and died," Brenda repeated with disbelief.

"Michael came by to tell Cora those Gangster Disciples are going to try and kill her because their friend died early this morning," Laura said. "They blame Cora. They think she poisoned him."

Brenda looked as if she might faint. "How did Michael know that?"

"He overheard a conversation between Reverend Benson and two of the gang members," Nebia said. "The reverend's been trying to put them boys on the right road, but it's obvious it didn't work."

Brenda's eyes fluttered. "None of this can be true. It can't."

"It's as true as your standing here," Laura said. "All of it. And them threatening to kill Cora is real, too. Michael told us they plan to do it by tomorrow morning. So he helped us convince Cora that she's got to leave. Go back to Africa." Laura wiped her eyes. "He was heading to the bank to get money for Cora and Faith's airplane tickets when he had the heart attack."

Brenda slumped down and Cora caught her and helped her to the couch.

"I know this is hard," Cora said in her ear. "God knows, I know this feels unbearable."

Brenda began to cry, but it had no sound. Her mouth opened wide, but nothing came out but torrents of tears. Finally, she turned slowly and looked at everyone. "I just found out that I'm pregnant."

Cora sat down beside Brenda and drew her in her arms. They cried together. Brenda was the first to pull back.

"I gotta go to the hospital. Maybe Michael didn't die." She wiped her face. "But first I'm going to write you a blank check." Brenda looked at Cora. "Cash it at our bank. Write it for whatever you need to make your trip."

Cora and Brenda looked deep into each other's eyes. They hugged again.

Brenda stood up. "I've got to go."

"You shouldn't go alone," Cora said.

"What are you going to do? Come with me?" Brenda shook her head. "You don't have time for that. And Michael was my husband." Her thumb hit her chest. "I want to do this alone."

Cora looked down. "Yes. I understand."

Brenda lifted Cora's chin. "But it's so good to be back. To show I love my sister again. Even in the middle of all of this." Brenda looked at Laura. "It's so good to be back."

Two large tears made their way from the corners of Laura's eyes. She opened her arms to Brenda. Brenda went down on her knees and into her mother's arms. "Mama. Mama."

"I love you, child. I love you."

Cora covered her face and cried silently in her hands.

Finally, Brenda rose to her feet. She hugged Nebia and Cora. "We'll see each other again."

"Of course we will," Cora replied. "Once this stuff is over I'll be back. I just don't want nobody else to be hurt because of me. But I intend to come back."

"Where's Faith?" Brenda asked.

"She's napping upstairs." Cora glanced at the stairway. "I'll have to get her up soon enough."

"Here, Brenda." Laura dug into her pocket. "You take this key, and come back here once you leave the hospital." Brenda clasped the key in her hand. "This isn't a time to be alone, no matter what you find out." Laura lifted her chin. "We're your family. And we're here for you if you need us."

Nebia nodded.

"Thank you," Brenda said through fresh tears. "But I know Michael's gone." She wrote the check and handed it to Cora. "He's gone. I can feel it." She looked off. "And maybe, finally, he'll have some peace. No matter what I did, and no matter how I tried to make him love me the way he loved you, Cora, I never could."

"Brenda, don't," Cora said.

"But it's the truth. It was my greatest fear from the moment we married. And I threw it up in his face often enough. But this is the first time that I ever really accepted it myself." Brenda looked down. "And maybe it's selfish of me that it comes at this moment, at a moment when I know I will never have to share him with you again." Brenda smiled a sad smile and went to her car.

Nebia's Story . . .

"Damn," Sheila said. "Michael died, too."

"With a heart attack. Not too far from the house. The car ran into a telephone pole," Nebia said.

"The timing sure is interesting," Cynthia replied. "It's like he died from heartache or heartbreak because Cora was leaving. Wow. That was some mixed-up stuff."

"It was a draining time," Nebia said.

"But Laura and Brenda finally made up," Erica said.

Nebia nodded. "That was something to see. Something to see."

"So was Cora and Faith able to leave safely?"

"They left all right. Right in the knick of time."

Chapter 33

Carefully, Nebia pulled the car over to the curb in front of the airport. She sat looking straight ahead.

"I guess there's no need to make this worse than it already is," Cora said softly as she turned to Nebia, who sat beside her.

"I guess not." Nebia looked at her with tears in her eyes.

"Nebia, don't you dare cry," Cora said. "If you cry, how can I go? How can I go if you cry?" She threw her arms around Nebia.

Faith moved toward them from the back. She slid her slim body between the two front seats. "Grandma Nebia, you crying?" Her tiny hands patted Nebia's head.

"No child. Of course not." Nebia blinked several times. "You're going with your mother to Africa. There's going to be lots of things to see there, big animals and I hear it's beautiful." Nebia smiled into Faith's pudgy face. "But you got to promise Grandma Nebia one thing."

"What's that, Grandma Nebia?"

"You'll always think of me when you see a giraffe."

"That's the one with the long neck?" Faith's tender brow wrinkled.

Nebia nodded. "That's right."

"But you don't have a long neck, Grandma Nebia. I can hardly see your neck at all." She leaned her head to the side.

"But I've always held my head high and kept my eyes open, and sometimes I can see what others can't. I want you to be that way, Faith."

Faith nodded, although she looked uncertain; then she sat back as Cora got out of the car and opened the back door.

She leaned inside and hugged her mother as Nebia walked to the back of the vehicle. "Bye, Mama."

"Bye, Sugar," Laura replied. "You take care of yourself and this baby. You hear? I'll see you when you come back," she added without conviction.

"Yes, you will." Cora looked into her eyes. "I love you, Mama."

"You know I've always loved you, Cora," Laura replied.

Cora wiped her eyes and reached for Faith. The child climbed into her arms. "Say good-bye to Grandma. Give her a hug," she coaxed.

"Bye, Gran'ma."

"Bye, baby. Bye." Laura pulled Faith to her chest as Cora held onto her waist. Finally, Laura let go. Afterwards she sat staring at her lap.

"Come with Mama," Cora said as she put Faith down. She walked to the trunk of the car and removed two suitcases. "I guess this is it." Cora inhaled. She hugged Nebia again. "Thank you." Her voice broke. "Thank you for everything."

Nebia broke the hold. "You just get on inside that airport."

As dusk descended, Cora motioned for a skycap, and with Faith holding an old doll, she walked toward the entrance of the airport.

"Take care of yourself," Nebia yelled.

Cora turned, waved, touched her heart, and they disappeared inside.

* * *

Brenda was waiting when Nebia and Laura arrived home. "Michael is gone," she said through soft tears. "I'm going to make all the arrangements tomorrow. That's if I can."

Nebia patted Brenda's back.

"We'll help you, child. Don't you worry." Laura took her hand.

"You look so tired, Nebia," Brenda said.

"I am tired. Not just my body but my heart's tired too," Nebia replied.

"Is Cora gone?"

"She will be in about an hour," Laura said.

Nebia rubbed her eyes. "Think I'll go on upstairs and lay down for a minute."

"It's probably a good idea for both of you to rest," Brenda said. "I'll stay up front here. Maybe I'll look at T.V. or something. But right now"—she paused—"I just don't want to be alone."

"There's no need to be." Laura patted her arm. "You stay here as long as you need to. This is your home."

"Mama," Brenda said softly.

"Mm?"

"I hate that Cora's gone now that we could finally be together. I feel like I've missed the opportunity."

"They'll be another," Laura replied, but Nebia just looked down and left the room.

"I think I will go to my room and lay down." Laura struggled to turn the wheelchair around. "I'm feeling a little drained."

Brenda came over and began to push the chair.

"No, that's all right. I can make it." Laura propelled herself forward. "I've made it through Annette's death. I can make it through anything."

Brenda watched her mother leave the room. Then she turned and gazed at the odds and ends that she remembered from childhood. She touched things and opened drawers. It was in a drawer that Brenda came across the only photo album her mother owned. She took it to the couch and opened it.

There were baby pictures, and snapshots when they were little girls. The three of them together—she, Cora, and Annette. Annette was always in the middle, and Cora always looked like she had something better to do. Brenda touched her own image, standing straight and tall. There was a photo of a shapely, statuesque Laura wearing a fancy hat and a pretty dress, taken right before church in her church days. Brenda shook her head at all the changes time had wrought.

A soft click interrupted the memories and Brenda looked up. The sound came again, but this time the doorknob turned and three men wearing stocking cap masks burst inside.

They stood and looked at her.

"Where is your sister?" one of them demanded.

"She's not here." Brenda got up.

"Where is she?" he repeated.

"She's gone. She's not here."

"You by yourself?"

Brenda kept her eyes on his face. "Yes. I'm here alone. My mother's at the grocery store with the woman upstairs. They'll be back any minute, so you better leave."

"We not leaving here without getting some revenge for T-Mac."

"What are you talking about?"

"Your sister killed him. That's what I'm talking about. The bitch poisoned him."

"That's not true." Brenda shook her head. "Cora wouldn't do that."

"It doesn't matter to me if you believe it or not." He stuck his chin out. "Either way someone's going to pay for my brother, T-Mac, dying."

"Pay for it?" Brenda started to cry. "Hasn't enough damage been done already?" Angrily, she swiped at her tears. "Somebody killed Warren, Cora's husband. Somebody stabbed him and he died. Have you considered God may have gotten his payback with T-Mac's death?"

"I don't believe in no God anyway. Yeah, T-Mac killed that policeman. I don't know if your God had something to do with it or not, but I'm God tonight." He made a fake lunge forward.

Startled, Brenda knocked over one of Laura's ceramic figurines.

"And it looks like it's going to be you that I play God on." He went and stood in front of the kitchen door. Then he spread his arms wide.

Brenda stiffened. "If you're so determined to take another life . . . I don't know what I can do to stop you. All I know is, there's so much sadness in my heart I'm not going to fight you. I'm not going to fight you at all. And maybe you'll remember what I'm about to say." She shook her head. "I'm in no position to fight you. I don't have the strength." Brenda looked at each one of them. "My husband died today because of this. All of this"—her arm circled—"is tied together. All this death, sadness and grief. When will it end?"

"Man, what you about to do?" One of the others spoke up. "This lady didn't do nothin' to us."

"No, she didn't," T-Mac's brother replied. "But her sister's not here and before I leave, somebody's going to get what I came to give. Somebody's going to die because my brother's dead."

"But maybe she's right. Maybe we just need to let it go, man. Three people are dead now. Death is everywhere."

"I ain't lettin' nothin' go. If you a coward and you want to walk out of here, go!" T-Mac's brother pointed to the other man. "You too, for that matter. Y'all just go right ahead. But I got to take care of this. I got to take care of it for T-Mac."

Brenda turned her back and began to sing "His Eye Is On The Sparrow."

"This is for the T," T-Mac's brother declared.

"Don't you hurt my child!" Laura's scream cut the air. She stood on one leg with her arm drawn back. A syringe was in her fist.

"Mama!" Brenda turned just as the front door burst open and several policemen entered the house. Nebia was behind them.

"Put your hands up. You three are under arrest," one of the officers said.

"Nebia!" Laura dropped the syringe and leaned against the wall. "Thank God."

Brenda rushed to her mother's side.

"I saw them snooping around the side of the house when I was about to go inside my place," Nebia said. "I knew they were going to try to get in here, so I called the police."

"We had just received a phone call from Pastor Benson warning us that something like this might happen," the head officer said.

The police officers handcuffed the gang members.

"And we heard the whole thing," the officer in charge continued. "We know T-Mac killed Warren." He jerked up on T-Mac's brother's handcuffs. "Now we got something that will keep you behind bars, and with you and your brother off the streets, maybe things will calm down in this neighborhood."

Laura was very unsteady. She had not stood in years.

"Hold on, Mama." Brenda went for the wheelchair. She positioned it behind Laura, who collapsed into the seat.

"Take them out of here," the main officer commanded. "Miss Nebia, we've got to take some police reports. You want to come outside? We'll start with you."

"All right," Nebia said. She looked over at Brenda and Laura.

"Thank you. All of you," Brenda said as they started through the door.

"Yes. We can't thank you enough," Laura added, out of breath.

When the door closed behind them Brenda asked, "You okay, Mama?"

"I'm fine. You?"

"I'm all right."

They stared at each other.

"You would have killed that man, wouldn't you?" Brenda said.

"Yes, I would have." Laura's eyes took on a distant look. "I would have killed him dead without a second thought."

Brenda's face trembled. "All these years we've wasted." She touched her mother's shoulders. "I'm going to make it up to you,

Mama." Brenda paused. "You can move in with me if you like. But I don't ever want us to be like we were again." She knelt down and placed her head in Laura's lap.

"You don't have to worry about that, child. It was more my fault than it ever was yours." Laura stroked Brenda's hair.

"Oh, Mama. Why does life have to be so hard? Why did we have to go through so much to come together?"

"Who knows, other than God? And who says God thinks like us? He's the one that's got the big picture." Laura sniffed. "He took little Annie so early. But she never seemed to be of this earth anyway. And Warren, who only tried to do good because he never felt he fit anywhere. And Michael. Poor Michael. He loved this family so much it consumed him."

"Now all of them are gone." Brenda looked up at Laura. "Cora's gone, too."

"Yes. Cora's gone." Laura sighed. "But when you and I look at each other, we know no matter where Cora is, we'll always be family."

Brenda nodded and laid her head in Laura's lap again.

Nebia's Story . . .

There were sniffles all around the porch. Tears streamed down Erica's face, and Cynthia wiped away the few that had fallen. Sheila simply sat with her eyes closed.

Nebia stopped rocking and looked at her hands.

"What happened to the Robinsons after that, Miss Nebia?" Sheila asked.

"Laura died when Brenda's baby was six months old. And eventually Brenda and her little boy moved to Washington, D.C. It's her property management company that takes care of this building and the other houses she and Michael owned." Nebia looked off into the distance. "I understand that just about every year, they go to Africa."

"Brenda never asked you to go with them," Erica said, looking disappointed, "as close as you were?"

"Who said she didn't?" Nebia gave Erica a sideways look. "Traveling like that is not for me. And now, at my age—I'm one hundred and one—I'm too old to travel. But I'm too young for a tomb."

Cynthia looked at Sheila, and Erica looked down.

"Did Cora ever come back?" Cynthia asked.

"No." Nebia rose from her chair and walked to the door of her apartment.

"You knew she wasn't coming back, didn't you?' Erica asked with respect.

Nebia looked at her. "Yes, I knew. But after all these years there's one thing that gives me comfort."

"What is that?" Erica asked.

Nebia held up a solid fist. "When everything was said and done, in their hearts the Robinsons were like this. That's what brings me peace." She opened her door and disappeared inside.